Health, Heart, and Pocketbook

The Ernie Jackson Story
as told by
Ernie Jackson

Copyright © 2022 Ernest Jackson, Jr.

All rights reserved. The unauthorized reproduction or distribution of this copyrighted work, in whole or part, in any form by any electronic, graphics mechanical, including photocopying recording, taping or by any information storage retrieval system or other means, is illegal and forbidden, without the written permission of the publisher. The information contained within this book is strictly for educational purposes. If you wish to apply ideas contained in this book, you are taking full responsibility for your actions. The author has made every effort to ensure the accuracy of the information within this book was correct at the time of publication. The author does not assume and hereby disclaims any liabilities to any party for any loss, damage, or disruption caused by errors or omission result from accident, negligence, or any other cause.

Colored Mirrors Publishing, LLC

4008 Louetta Road, Ste 193

Spring, TX 77388

www.coloredmirrorspublishing.com

coloredmirrorspublishing@gmail.com

Cover Picture: Ernie Jackson – At Prairie View A&M, in 2014.

Editor: Atossa McCrary

Book Design: Darshell McAlpine

Health, Heart, and Pocketbook

ISBN: 978-1-73210-784-7

Library of Congress: 2022933055

Contents

Acknowledgments	vii
Tributes	ix
Foreword	xiii
Introduction	xv
CHILDHOOD	1
The Extraordinary Rosie Mae Jackson	1
Growing up Black in a Small White Town	3
My Heroes Growing Up	6
High School Years in Upstate New York	9
Basketball Saves the Day	11
FIRSTS OF ADULTHOOD	15
First Job . . . First Love	15
The Path out of Insanity	17
A New Direction	19
Black Students Takeover Willard Straight Hall	21
Campus Unrest Shocks the Nation	23
Life in the Fast Lane	24
EJ SMOKE	27
EJ Smoke Is Born	27
Broadcasting and Photography Changes Everything	28
Farewell to New York State	32
Opportunity in South Carolina	35
RADIO MAJIC	39
America's Oldest Black Radio Station	39
Broken Radio Stations in Norfolk Virginia	46
Majicman and a Photography Career Merge	48
The Majic Is Back	50
One Childhood Dream Comes True	52
The Houston Radio War Ends	54

HOUSTON RADIO MAKES HISTORY	59
I love My Job Barbecue Contest	60
Majic 102 Gas Sale	61
Pay Your Bill	62
The Story of Jerry Canty	62
Haiti-Rwanda Relief Effort	63
The Story of Jamie Green	63
MLK (30th Anniversary Assassination) Celebration	64
Roll to the Polls	65
Testing for Tickets	67
ENDINGS	69
End of a Broadcast Career	69
Who Killed Black Radio?	75
NEW BEGINNINGS	79
Project W.A.V.E Goes to the Big Apple	79
Destiny's Child Steps Up for Project W.A.V.E.	81
Together Rx Access	84
Beans4Good	87
AGAIN IN RADIO	91
Trouble at KTSU-FM	91
Back in the Saddle Again	94
HAVE CAMERA WILL TRAVEL	99
Life as a Photographer	99
National Parks	103
Notes	131
RECOGNITIONS	137
References	151

This book is dedicated to my mother Rosie Mae Jackson, whom you will read about in the very first chapter of the book. An incredibly strong, yet gentle woman, she raised three children in a small, all-White town in upstate, 1950s New York. She was beloved by everyone who knew her. It was her guidance and example that made me the person I am today.

Acknowledgments

I want to thank Sonyia Graham, a colleague and lifelong friend who inspired and motivated me to write this book. It was her constant support and encouragement that made it possible. I want to thank all my friends and co-workers who supported me in my twenty-eight-year career in radio, in my HIV/AIDS, Together RX Access initiatives, and at Cornell University: Parker Jenkins, Bill Gerich, Samantha Choice, Julia Bonney, Bob Davis, Cindy Webster, Janet Armstand, and so many more.

Most, I want to thank my wife, Willda Shaw Jackson, who put up with me for forty-seven years. Thank you also to my sister Norma Jean, my brother Patrick, my five sons, and all my nieces, nephews, grandchildren, great-nieces, and great-nephews, and my one great-grandnephew.

Tributes

When it comes to Black radio, I can think of no better champion for its intrinsic value than Ernest Jackson. Working alongside Ernie for several years at MAJIC-102 FM in Houston, I witnessed his unapologetic commitment to the use of Black radio to support the community. E.J. believed it was incumbent upon Black radio stations to be more than just sources of entertainment and platforms for musical talent who had been denied general market airplay, but for it to, more importantly, be a catalyst to educate and inform.

He used radio as an advocacy tool, a voice for the underserved, and a face for the unseen. And he did so with the aplomb and diplomacy of a seasoned legislator. At its best, Ernie considered Black radio the "soil" to nourish the grassroots of a thriving community.

—**Selma Dodson Tyler**

Ernie and I had been friends since the early nineties. I arrived in Houston in 1980, he arrived in 1993, and we both are from the northeast. Our paths crossed as a result of my work as a regional marketing manager for a restaurant chain with fifty-two locations while he was the driving force that built Majic 102 into the powerhouse radio of the gulf coast. Ernie knew he was the voice of Black Houston. As the radio leader to chase, he also knew how to move the needle: what to say and how to say it. He was the engineer of persuasive impact radio.

He cultivated relationships well. He invited his customers to judge BBQ cook-offs and to be guests in his outdoor events. He was clever in his approach, giving you something before he asked you for something. Ernie understood knowledge was more powerful than money.

During the early nineties, Houston was in transition after the savings and loan crisis and oil bust. It was on the rise. We had referendums to build hotels, stadiums, and arenas. Using taxpayer money required citywide votes. So, with Ernie's help, a group of us worked to gather those votes. In this group included community leaders, who had been public allies championing contracting and entrepreneurship as the way for our community to pull itself up. We needed to own our businesses and to hire our own people.

This collaboration strategy and radio airway takeover impact were massive. From here on, Ernie Jackson became the "wizard behind the curtain." Ernie was directly responsible for Lee Brown becoming the first Black mayor of Houston. His radio spots had such persuasive impact, and he was the master of in-your-face journalism radio, the "Malcolm X of Radio." He knew he had the power to move the entire Black population, and he did it over and over again. The 1100 room Hilton Hotel, Toyota Center, and Minute Maid Park all had major minority participation. Having fifty Black millionaires in Houston resulted from the efforts that would never have happened without Ernie Jackson.

In the last few years, Ernie and I would talk two to three times a week. He lamented the fact that TSU Radio is nearly completely insignificant in this market. He even joined the board to improve the operation and content, but the fact that Black Houston did not have what it should have in TSU radio presence bothered him. He was an advocate of his community, yet he did not suffer fools or foolishness. We often talked about Houston politics, about stool softeners, about our dogs. Like two old men sitting on the porch, we pontificated about all manner of things: good coffee, Black folks, and travel.

As Ernie lay there on the last day of his journey, we realized his battle was over. He had fought a good fight. Willda, Sonyia, and I chatted as if he was talking back to us. We stayed with Willda to comfort her, and we knew Ernie expected that of us. Still stunned, knowing that the maverick, once the voice of the Black community, the wizard and Malcolm X of Black radio, quietly died.

Well . . . Ernie, with his magnificent voice and actions and dedication to his village, carved his name into the *Tree of Life*. Simply said: Ernie was here. Rest well, my brother. We kept our promise. We did not forget. We let them know, Ernie was here.

—**Darryl King**: CEO & Member, PPG Global, LLC

Ernest Jackson was a man with the passion, vision, and ambition to bring social equity and justice to those who deserved to be seen and heard. His unique blend of knowledge in public health and radio broadcasting served well in the development and realization of the nationally acclaimed HIV/Aids testing and outreach program known as Project W.A.V.E. I was honored to be included in his efforts and success.

—**Mike Vogel**: Former Director of Government Affairs at DuPont Pharmaceuticals

They say when we Black folks die and go to heaven, it's not going to be Saint Peter who meets us at the pearly gates. Rather, it will be a group of our ancestors—our ancestors who were formerly enslaved. And they will have one question for each of us, and one question only. That is: what have you done with your freedom?

Rest assured, when Ernie Jackson got to those gates last year, the ancestors didn't have to ask him that question. They knew. This was Ernest Jackson—a man who absolutely made the most of his freedom. A man who lived to uplift his people and community. A man who truly made his ancestors proud. I believe that when the ancestors met

Ernie at the pearly gates, they just smiled at him and said: "Well done, brother! Well done."

Ernest Jackson was a rare human being—the kind of person who elevated the humanity of every individual he met. He led by example and showed others how this life can be best lived: with love, courage, grace, style, and his trademark megawatt smile. In short, Ernest Jackson was a man to truly admire, a man who I can truly say made me a better person.

Thank you Ernie, for your friendship, your love, your guidance, and your wisdom. Thank you for the opportunity to be your friend and fellow artist. Thank you for showing me light at those moments I was consumed by darkness. I miss you every day, my brother. I try every day to live up to your example.

Ernie's memoir reads like a road map to life, showing us all how we can live our best lives. May we all take inspiration from Ernie's amazing life. In these pages and in our hearts, he lives on.

—**Mustapha Khan**: 2022, New York

Foreword

I was referred to Ernie by Cindy Webster to provide promotional products for Project W.A.V.E. I was quickly captivated by Ernie's genuine spirit to serve his community and make a difference. I remember asking him about some beautiful photos on display in his office, blown away when he mentioned these were photos he took as a hobby. My thoughts were that they would make some beautiful postcards. Over the thousands of pictures Ernie took in his lifetime, he selected a few of his favorite to share in this book. Ernie and I shared a love of entrepreneurship, and no matter how nonconventional the business concept, we knew the other was on board.

Over the years, through the many stories of his life that he shared with me, I soon came to understand just how much history about Black radio I and many others did not know. Ernie not only played a pinnacle part in radio, but he is also the reason several major things came to be in Houston. Things that would not have been if there wasn't an Ernest Jackson Jr.

I wanted the world to know his story. So I nagged him to write this book to share his amazing life and contributions. Soon all the planets lined up, and it just so happened his son Matthew and his daughter-in-law gifted him Storyworth, which gave him an outline and direction to begin writing his biography.

Those who knew Ernie knew his love of sports. So getting edits during March Madness was absolutely not happening, but up until his last trip to the hospital in April, Ernie was finalizing his book.

Ernie passed away a few weeks later, on April 30, 2021, but he left us with his legacy: "Health, Heart, and Pocketbook."

I am truly honored that Ernie trusted me to publish and share his legacy with you.

I miss you, my lifelong friend and entrepreneurial partner in crime.

—Sonyia Baring Graham

Introduction

Health, Heart, and Pocketbook is a call to action, a guide to remind us what is important, a blueprint for success!

When I arrived in Memphis, Tennessee in 1983, I was forty years old, so it was a bit unusual to have a mentor at that age. Yet, I had Charles "Mr. Chuck" Scruggs, who was born in 1932 in Chattanooga, Tennessee. He got his start in radio at age sixteen as the host of his own R&B show. He attended Tennessee State University where he helped to establish the school's first radio station. He was the first Black general manager at WDIA: the oldest Black radio station in America.

Chuck had called me to come to Memphis to become the sales manager for WDIA. What he hadn't told me at the time was that his intention was for me to be the general manager all along. One year later when I was promoted to general manager, I became the second Black general manager and only the third general manager in the station's forty-year history. WDIA, at the time, was owned by Viacom Radio, a division of CBS. Viacom also owned KDIA in Oakland,

California, so I ended up the general manager and vice president for both stations.

Chuck had a slogan when talking about what the focus of WDIA should be in its music, news, promotions, and especially, in its community events. The slogan was: "Health, Heart, and Pocketbook." He said that was what WDIA's loyal listeners wanted and what they deserved from the station.

Whenever anyone would ask Chuck what he thought about an idea, he would just look at you and say, "Health, Heart, and Pocketbook." We immediately knew whether the idea was good or not. My mother taught us when we were having trouble making a decision to always follow our hearts. Chuck's motto for success and my mother's advice were the driving motivation for all the great things my staff and I achieved in twenty-eight years, at ten different radio stations, in six different cities. I hope you enjoy reading about it.

Childhood

The Extraordinary Rosie Mae Jackson

My mother was without a doubt the single most important and most influential person in my life, not only as a child but also as an adult. Rosie Mae Jackson was born November 13, 1913, in Gainesville, Texas. My sister and I grew up without a father as he and my mother had divorced when I was ten and my sister Norma Jean was nine.

My mother moved us from Texas to Upstate New York in 1953. We lived on Sampson Air Force Base near the small town of Ovid, New York, with my older sister Alma and her husband, Master Sergeant Wallace Dell. I don't remember much about life on base except for two things. First, my sister and I found out there was no Santa Claus, and like most people, we remember where we were when we found out.

It was also there that I got my first job: shining shoes. I did well because we were living in a place where *spit-shined* shoes were the protocol. Two years after arriving at Sampson, Sergeant Dell was sent on a three-year tour of duty to Japan. No longer dependents, we had to move off the base.

We found a small house in Lodi Point, New York. It overlooked Seneca Lake, the largest of the beautiful Finger Lakes. Now as a landscape photographer, I think walking to the school bus each morning with that beautiful lake in my eyes triggered my appreciation for nature and the outdoors.

It was there that I also found my second job selling nightcrawlers. Nightcrawlers are very large earthworms that come out after dark and lie on the wet grass. My mother and I used to grab them and pull them out of the ground. I would keep them in cans and sell them to fishermen who passed our house on the way to the lake. My mother loved to fish, and we often drove the mile and a half down the hill to the lake ourselves. My mother kept every fish she caught regardless of the size. She always said, "If this fish is big enough to get on my hook, then it's big enough to eat."

Everyone, of course, knew us because our color was conspicuous. We were the only African American family in Lodi Point, and also Ovid, the town where my sister and I commuted fifteen miles to get to school. My mother was beloved by everyone in both these two small towns. Everyone knew Rosie.

Sargent Dell had left my mother his car, an Oldsmobile Eighty-Eight, and it was our transportation all over Upstate New York. There wasn't a back road anywhere around there that Rosie didn't know about. We spent our weekends traveling to the incredible parks and lakes in the area, with Rosie's heavy foot along for the ride. There were times when we would be riding along the back roads; she would get pulled over by a state trooper. After the officer pulled her over, he would walk up to the window of our car, and my mother would roll down the window.

The officer would say, "Good afternoon, Rosie. Where are you headed?"

My mother would answer, "Oh just headed back to Lodi Point," or to wherever we were going at the time.

The officer would then reply, "Okay, Ms. Jackson. You slow down now and have a nice day."

In all the time we lived there (nearly fifteen years), I never saw Rosie get a speeding ticket.

My mother had worked at Sampson Air Force Base as the head cook at the NCO (Non-Commissioned Officers) Club. And boy could she cook! After we moved to Lodi Point, there wasn't much work in that area for my mother. She decided to work for Seneca County keeping foster children. You will hear more about the wonderful lady who raised three children in the 1950s in a small town in rural Upstate New York, absent of "colored folk" for miles and miles.

Growing up Black in a Small White Town

Most of my childhood and my teen years were spent doing things outside: exploring wooded areas, riding a sled down big gullies in winter, building a fort in the woods, fishing, and of course, selling nightcrawlers.

Our mother had two close friends who lived not too far from us. One, Miss Hanky, raised chickens and sold eggs. Our mother would take us with her when she went to buy eggs. On one occasion, we begged Miss Hanky for a baby chick. She was happy to give us one, and we were excited to have a pet. We named the chick Eric. It turned out Eric was a rooster not a hen, and we played with him in our yard.

My sister was afraid of Eric because she thought he was going to bite her. Eric knew she was afraid, and so he always chased her. In fact, almost every day when we got off the school bus, Eric would be waiting for Jean and would chase her into the house. This went on for a few years. One day when we arrived home from school, Eric was not there to greet us. We wondered where he was, but when we asked our mother, she told us she had not seen Eric.

In addition to eggs, my mother bought chickens from Miss Hanky. She made fried chicken, baked chicken, stewed chicken, and the most incredible chicken potpie. On the day we came home and could not find Eric, we were told that we were having chicken for dinner. When we sat down at the table, our mother brought in a chicken that did not look like any chicken we had ever seen her cook; it did not look good. I looked at my sister, she looked at me, and we both knew what had happened to Eric. Neither one of us ate that night. It was probably the only night in our lives that we went to bed hungry. Our mother denied, for the rest of her life, ever cooking Eric, but we knew better.

Upstate New York and The Finger Lakes had long and very harsh winters. A few years after we moved to Lodi Point, we had a severe snowstorm that dropped over three feet of snow over a four-day period. Everything was closed! Grocery stores, schools, hospitals, and every road within a hundred miles. Our house was heated by a fuel oil furnace, delivered each month by a delivery truck. Because the roads were closed the truck could not deliver fuel to us. It was a neighbor who brought us fuel on a wagon attached to a snowmobile. That fuel had to be dropped from a helicopter about twenty miles from where we lived.

My sister had severe asthma and was sick a lot during the long winters. This was 1960 in Ovid, New York, and doctors were still making house calls. I still remember Dr. Allen, the local doctor, administering treatment to Norma.

The summer after the big snowstorm, I got my first real job. It was a job helping a local farmer store hay. I worked in the loft of a big barn stacking hay from a conveyer belt; the job lasted one day. After I got home, I was sick as a dog: sneezing, coughing, wheezing, eyes running, head aching. That's how I found out I had hay fever. The next house visit from Dr. Allen was for me. For the next few summers, I found jobs picking fruit: cherries, apples, peaches, and grapes. The Finger Lakes are famous for their grape vineyards.

School was often a challenge for both my sister and me. Being the only Black kids in the school, we often had to listen to comments about niggers, or listen to nigger jokes. Although they were not always directed at us, we tried to ignore the fact that we heard them.

One of the worst experiences occurred in my geography class. One Friday, our teacher asked us to come back on Monday and tell where our ancestors came from. The year was 1959. A time when the worst stereotypes of Black people and African people were alive and well. Most of our classmates and society as a whole thought all Africans were like those portrayed in Tarzan movies. I thought the same. I was scared to death all weekend thinking about having to go to class that Monday, and when asked where my ancestors had come from, I would have to say Africa.

When my turn came that Monday and the teacher called on me, I could hardly get the words Africa out of my mouth. In fact, the teacher had to ask me to repeat my answer. I was ashamed. Little did I know at that time, Africa and African people were not like what we saw in Tarzan movies. Africans were stolen from their homes, put in ships, chained, beaten, and sold into slavery when they arrived in America. These stolen people were kings, queens, doctors, and scholars in their own land.

It is ironic that years later I found out that my ancestors had actually come from the West Indies and not from Africa. It would be during the civil rights movement and the Black power movement that I would first come to identify with and appreciate the real nature of the African American struggle in America.

My Heroes Growing Up

Growing up, most of my heroes were people who I didn't know. They were heroes from a distance. My earliest recollection of a hero was a man who I thought was my father. My mother and father divorced when I was very young. The man I remember being around me was my Uncle Leon. My memories of him are vague, but later in life when I saw pictures of him, I discovered he looked a lot like my father. I remember him being around my sister and me when I was very young living in Texas. Later as a teenager and as a young adult, another of my heroes was my Uncle David Bennett.

I had four uncles and three aunts. The Uncles were Dave, Leon, Neal, and Edgle. My aunts were Hazel, Marie, and Lena Mae. Only Uncle Dave was ever a part of my life after we left Texas. He helped us move from Texas, and when my mother left New York after I graduated from high school, he helped her move to Chicago where Aunt Hazel lived. He lived in Washington, D.C. where he was a taxi driver, an avid golfer, and a hustler. I remember when he would visit us in New York, he would go out on the golf course and drive balls in every direction.

None of the balls he hit ever went straight. However, that only happened when there were other golfers around watching him. When the local golfers saw him, they would invite him to play a round or two (always with a few dollars being wagered). After that, everything he hit was not only straight but long as well. He won a lot of money on that golf course.

My mother had heroes that were also mine. Three of her heroes were members of the Brooklyn Dodgers baseball team. Don Newcomb, Roy Campanula, and Jackie Robinson. I am not sure how my mother ever became such an avid Brooklyn Dodgers fan. But maybe it was because the team had players who looked like her.

In 1955, three years after we moved to Upstate New York, we

attended a baseball game at historic Ebbets Field in Brooklyn. Don Newcombe was pitching that day, and sometime during that game, Roy Campanella hit a long home run. My mother was so excited she threw her purse up in the air, and we never were able to find it.

I grew up as a teen listening to another of my childhood heroes, Milo Hamilton. Milo was the radio play-by-play announcer for the Chicago White Sox during my last years in high school. I would listen to Milo on the Chicago station WCFL. I could hear the station all evening in Ovid; it was what is known as a *clear-channel* station.

Clear-channel stations were radio stations that were designated by the FCC (Federal Communications Commission) as the only stations on their particular dial position that could broadcast twenty-four hours a day.[1] Any other radio station with that dial position had to power down (cut their power) at sunset so that any clear-channel station at the dial position could be heard coast to coast. This was a part of the Communication Act passed by Congress in 1934, and clear-channel stations still exist today.

Forty years later, I met Milo Hamilton in person after I moved to Houston to run two radio stations owned by Clear Channel Radio. But that is a story for another day.

As a teenager and only Black student at Ovid High School, I didn't have many friends outside of those with whom I played sports. One exception to that was Ken Peterson. Ken was two or three years older than me. He attended Ovid High School, but he was absent from school more than he was present. I think he was suspended numerous times for various disciplinary reasons. His mother, Florence, was a dear friend of my mother's and was always coming to her rescue when times would get tough. Ken took me under his wing, and we had some great times together. They had lived not far from us after we later moved to Valois. Florence and my mother remained friends all their lives.

Growing up without a father during high school presented some challenging times for me. My mother was my rock, my inspiration, my teacher, my role model. She filled in at every opportunity when I needed a father for something important and sometimes not so important.

Another male in my life was my high school basketball, football, baseball, and track coach, James Biller. He coached me to be a better player, but he advised me and counseled me about so many other things in life throughout my high school years.

My last hero was a star lacrosse and football player who attended Syracuse University from 1953 to 1956; his name is Jim Brown. Jim Brown is considered by many people as the greatest running back to ever play football, and you can count me among those who think that.

Jim Brown was an award-winning lacrosse player from Manhasset Long Island who arrived at Syracuse University on a lacrosse scholarship in 1954. Syracuse University is about sixty-five miles from where I grew up in Ovid. Jim played lacrosse his freshman year at Syracuse. He was an All-American as a freshman, but because the game was so easy for him, he did little or nothing to stay in shape during the fall.

Lacrosse was a spring sport unlike football, which of course was a fall sport. The lacrosse coach at Syracuse asked Ben Schwartzwalder, who was the football coach at Syracuse, to let Brown work out with the football team during the fall to help him stay in shape for spring lacrosse, and the rest is history! In his senior year playing football, he was a consensus first team All-American and finished fifth in the Heisman Trophy voting.

Growing up so close to Syracuse University, I always wanted to see Jim Brown play in person. On the day of his final football game, I decided to hitchhike to Syracuse to see him play. As a teenager, I would often hitchhike to get to wherever I needed to go. I will never forget that rainy, windy day I decided to head to see Jim Brown play. It took me almost four hours to get to Syracuse and the campus. Syracuse was playing Colgate that day. Jim Brown and his Syracuse squad beat Colgate 61–7. Jim Brown rushed for 197 yards, scored six touchdowns, and kicked seven extra points in his final game at Syracuse. He remains one of my heroes to this day.

High School Years in Upstate New York

School at Ovid High School was always challenging. I didn't know it at the time, but it also taught me a set of life skills that would help me accomplish many good things. All the outside school activities for my sister and me centered around things we did at home. Still, I continued selling nightcrawlers and picked up jobs during the summer raking leaves for families who lived near us. My mother and I continued to fish as often as we could. It only took us a few minutes to drive to our favorite fishing spot at Lodi Point. My sister, however, never fished. Among other things, she didn't like putting worms on a hook. She was never available to help my mother and me catch nightcrawlers. Instead, we helped our mother plant, weed, and pick things from the garden.

Rosie grew mustard greens, turnip greens, beets, carrots, onions, and sometimes cabbage each year. We had some of the greatest meals with those foods. My favorites were greens, mustard and turnip cooked together, hot water cornbread, and chicken potpie. We had two giant cherry trees in the front of our house at Lodi Point, one with sweet cherries and one with sour cherries. I remember each year in late summer when the cherries got ripe, Jean and I used to make ourselves sick eating too many.

Just before I entered ninth grade at Ovid High, my mother moved us from Lodi Point to a house in Valois, about fifteen miles further south on Seneca Lake. We never knew why she moved us. The bus rides to school increased by fifteen to twenty minutes. It was a bigger house, but I didn't like it as much as Lodi Point. Instead of fuel oil for heat, we had coal. Someone would deliver coal through a passageway to our basement where the furnace was and where the coal was stored. I hated going down there to shovel coal to keep the house warm.

We didn't stay there long because basketball became a major part of my life at age sixteen. I was tall and showed some athletic ability after I reached fifteen and was recruited to play basketball for the junior varsity team. The team was outstanding, and during my sophomore year, our team won the league's championship.

The next year, when I became a varsity team member, getting home from practice became an issue. There was no late bus to get me from school in Ovid to Valois some forty minutes away. Hopes were high during my junior year that our team would win a basketball conference championship. Before the start of my junior year, my mother moved us to an Ovid house that was a ten-minute walk to my high school.

Life was good in Ovid! Moving there made us feel like we were living in a city. Even though it wasn't, it seemed like a city to us, after living in very rural Valois and Lodi Point. Up until the move to Ovid, we had been the only Black family in the county, but now we were also the only Black family in town. Rosie Mae Jackson had been loved and respected by everyone in Lodi Point and Valois. But she became a superstar when we moved into Ovid. I remember shortly after we moved into town my mother sent my sister and me to Dick Hughes Meat Market to purchase groceries. She sent us with a list: ground beef, chicken, fresh ground chili meat, sausage, etc. She gave us the list but didn't give us any money. We didn't ask questions; we just headed to the store. When we got to there, Mr. Hughes greeted us, and we handed him the paper. He looked it over, gathered all the items, put them into two large bags, and handed them to us.

Still not quite sure how this had worked, as we started to the door, we saw Mr. Hughes pull out a notepad and write down all the items he'd given us. Rosie would *settle up* at some point with Mr. Hughes and that was how it worked for Rosie Jackson. She had the same arrangement with Mr. Walter Lynd at the hardware store, Mr. Coke, the TV repairman, and Dr. Allen, who made the house calls. Who knows who else she had the same arrangements with?

Basketball Saves the Day

My final two years in high school were totally about sports. While most of my friends were also involved in sports, unlike me, they were also involved in the pursuit of romance. Romance was certainly on my agenda but was never a part of my routine. There were several girls in school whom I liked a lot, and I suspect one or two of them liked me as well. However, the stigma of liking and being the girlfriend of "the negro" in school prevented any of those young ladies from ever being a girlfriend, despite my star athlete status. I suspect my sister who was a year younger than me had the same issues, although we never talked about it. It was also around this time that another person joined our family.

My mother earned a living keeping foster children. During my last two years in school, she kept a couple of brothers named Michael and Billy Johnson. Billy was a terror: stole from my mother, fought in school constantly, and was eventually kicked out of school. My mother had to return him to Human Services. At about that same time, my mother took a one-year-old into her care, and his name was Patrick. My mother loved all the children under her care, even Billy, but there was something special about her relationship with young Patrick. Patrick had been abandoned by his mother and father. When someone inquired about the possibility of adopting him, my mother was heartbroken. She asked if there was any way she could keep Patrick, and keep him she did; she adopted him herself. I had never heard of a single mother being able to adopt a child, especially that young. Patrick never knew his biological mother, but he never needed to as Rosie Jackson was and always will be his mother.

During all this, I focused only on basketball and baseball. I was a superstar in basketball but only good in baseball. There was much anticipation during my senior year for us to win the league championship. After all, we had won the junior varsity one, and we had all our returning players healthy and ready for the upcoming season. The local newspaper had also predicted our success.

Our basketball coach was also our football and track coach. In the fall of my senior year, he suggested I play football to help me be in better shape for the upcoming basketball season. I will never forget the day I became a starting member of the football team. I was really just an average football player. I was lean and tall without much muscle mass. In those days, we played eight-men football, not eleven. There was a center, two guards, two ends, a quarterback, and two running backs. During an early practice before the season started, I was playing defense and found myself with an opportunity to tackle a running back who was headed around the end. I tackled him so hard he was stunned, and he did not immediately get up. Neither did I.

From that point on, I was the starting defensive back and wide receiver for the Ovid Hornets football team. I never made as hard a tackle as the one in practice. We won the championship, going undefeated. My final year in high school was the best of all the others. We started 8–0 in basketball, and as the star, I lead in scores and rebounds. I had an uncanny jumping ability that teammates and fans talked about before, during, and after every game. The ability was God-given, but when questioned about how I got it from others, I told people that I'd spent the summer shooting baskets in my backyard with galoshes on. Playing basketball with those really helped me improve. We lost the ninth game and ended the winning streak but went on to win the last six games to finish 14–1. I was named in the

Geneva Times Newspaper. I was the star of the team, of the town, of the whole county. But I still didn't have a girlfriend.

Because we won the championship, we qualified for the regional tournament that would eventually lead to a state tournament. We won our first regional game in overtime as I blocked the final shot to seal the deal. Our next opponent in the tournament was Lyons High School. They were a perennial powerhouse, having won the regional championship four of the five previous years. We faced them on a cold and snowy night in their home court. They had a six-foot, four-inch shooting guard by the name of Jim Boeheim. He had set every school scoring record during his time at Lyons High School, and he kicked our butts that night. He was unstoppable! We lost the game and were eliminated from the tournament. Both Jim Boeheim and I were named the all-regional tournament team, but I still didn't have a girlfriend.

Jim Boeheim became an all-star at the University of Syracuse. He roomed with future Hall of Fame player Dave Bing, which led Syracuse to its first-ever NCAA Basketball Tournament appearance. Ten years later, Boeheim became the university's head basketball coach and was inducted into the Hall of Fame winning over 900 games. When his team won its first-ever national championship game in New Orleans, I was there for that game. While walking down the street with my son Matthew, we passed Boeheim on his way back to his hotel. I recognized him and stopped to remind him about that game we'd played, and though he didn't remember me, he remembered the game. We shook hands, and the following night, he kicked Kansas' butts, just like he had done to us.

I graduated in May 1961, and I had no idea what was next for me. I had been offered a partial scholarship to Ithaca College which was just forty minutes away from Ovid. However, my mother didn't have the resources to pick up the rest of what it would have cost. So, like most of my classmates, I needed to look for a job. Ovid probably had a population of fewer than 2,000 people. My graduating class consisted of twenty-eight people, and there were not a lot of employment opportunities. The largest employer in the area was Willard State Hospital, a hospital for the mentally ill. Ironically, it had been a part of Sampson Air Force Base when we first moved to Upstate New York. They'd closed the base shortly after we moved to Lodi Point. I got a job at Willard State Hospital in summer 1961. A horrible incident happened one night and two days after I was hired. Some of my other classmates had also decided to go to work at Willard, and we were celebrating our joint hiring at the local bar, KT's. One of my classmates had a car and was driving all of us back from KT's.

It was a foggy night and visibility was very poor. As we rounded a curve, just three miles from my home, our driver hit and killed a man who looked like he was trying to cross the highway. Later, we found out he was a patient from Willard who had apparently wandered away from the hospital and was trying to find his way back. I started my first day, my first real job, the day after that accident. I didn't sleep for a week remembering the sound of the thud when our car hit that man.

Firsts of Adulthood

First Job . . . First Love

Since Ithaca and Geneva were forty minutes away, the largest two employers in the Ovid area were the Seneca Army Depot and Willard State Hospital. When we moved in with my sister Alma and her husband, the Sampson Air Base Hospital was the largest on any air force base in the United States. After the base closed, the hospital part was converted to Willard State Hospital. Most of my friends who did not go to college after graduation went to work at Willard. I was hired as a hospital attendant. It was at this time that my mother decided to leave Ovid and move to Chicago to be with my Aunt Hazel. She took my sister Jean and my brother Patrick with her. When she left, I was able to find very economical housing in an employee dorm at Willard.

I gave out medication, assisted patients with meals, made sure everyone bathed according to schedule, and sometimes broke up fights. Every patient in the hospital was assigned to a ward, which had dormitory-style sleeping arrangements and a large open space called the *day room*. Patients spent the day lounging, reading, sleeping, watching television, and fighting. Some wards at the hospital housed dangerous patients who were capable of harming themselves, other patients, and attendants. Many of them were locked in solitary confinement day and night, and we delivered meals through a small opening in the door. I was happy not to work in one of those wards. This was about the time that tranquilizer medications were being developed for use with the mentally ill: Thorazine being one of the first of those drugs. With the advent of those drugs, some who were in solitary confinement twenty-four hours a day were actually released during the daytime, and others could take on small jobs outside their ward.

By my second year into the job, I hated it. Then two things happen that changed things. I became friends with several of the more active patients, and I would take them on day trips outside. It was fun, but most of all it got me out of the deadly boring work. I proposed that the building management team create a position for me as recreational therapist over ten wards. They agreed. My days went from giving out pills and breaking up fights to taking patients outside, playing games, providing books, and doing other recreation.

Another change came outside the job. It was the sixties, and a new dance craze was sweeping the nation. It was called The Twist. There has never been a dance craze as popular as The Twist. Young folks, old folks, Black folks, White folks, doctors, lawyers, and Indian chiefs were all doing it. You know what they say about Black folks; they can dance, and I was a dancing machine, a twist phenom!

On Friday and Saturday nights, KT's, the hot spot in Willard, was filled with young White folks who had no rhythm, trying to do The Twist. On weekends, I walked in and danced the night away. I can remember dancing in front of a mirror at home to sharpen my moves. People from town came to KT's just to see me dance. I eventually bought a pair of Thom McAn, candy apple red, patent leather, zip-on shoes. And every Friday and Saturday night, I danced in them. I hardly ever had to buy myself a drink during those weekends. It was the local hangout, but we often had visiting nursing students who were on a two-month practicum.

One night, one of those young ladies walked in, bought me a drink, and asked me to dance. She was White, she was beautiful, and unlike her White friends, she could dance. Her name was Carol Houser. For the next two months, we spent every weekend together at KT's. It got to the point that when we took to the dance floor, everyone just watched us. I fell in love; it was my first love. Here I was a guy who'd never had a girlfriend in high school, hadn't taken anyone to the prom, and literally had never been kissed. When it came time for her to leave, she promised that we would continue to be in touch, but that didn't happen. For three weeks after she left, I called her every day but never got an answer, never got a return call. I decided to visit her at the school she attended to find out why. Geneseo State University was about a three-hour drive from Willard, and I made the trip unannounced.

When I arrived at her dorm, her roommate said she was not around, and she didn't want me to call her or visit her again. I was devastated. I remember the note I gave to her roommate to pass to her. It simply said, "Never have I traveled so far with such anticipation to be so disappointed." The first love of my life was gone after just four months.

The Path out of Insanity

Shortly after Ms. Carol Houser disappeared from my life, the other love of my life, my mother, also left for Chicago. Alone, I continued my job as an attendant at Willard, and as recreational therapist, I was no longer assigned to a particular ward, I met and interacted with a lot more patients and employees throughout the hospital. Later, I started to date one of the nurses: Sharon Warner. Second relationship, second nurse. She became pregnant not long after we started dating, and despite not really knowing each other that well, we decided to marry.

It was 1963, in Ovid, and with my family gone, I was the only Black person in town. We had a lot of trouble finding a minister who would marry us. After we found someone, we then had a hard time finding a place to live. The great ambassador Rosie Jackson was no longer around, and a lot of the goodwill toward her and me, left with her. So, Sharon rented a small house on her own, not letting on she was married and expecting a child. When the owner found out she was married to me and pregnant, he would not renew our lease. We decided to purchase a double-wide trailer, both fashionable and popular in that area, and bought a small plot to place the trailer.

On May 25, 1963, my first son, Terry, was born. Few things bring the kind of joy that the birth of a first child brings, especially a boy to a father. We adjusted as well as we could to life in Ovid, and we were generally accepted there.

I had become increasingly frustrated with Willard. It seemed to me there was no way to improve my lot in life or my job situation. All attendants on each ward reported to a supervisor, who were almost all male RNs.

I began to think about what it might take to become an RN and eventually a supervisor. I found out that the hospital had a two-year nursing program, where if you were approved, they would send you to school and pay your salary while studying. Later that year came one of the saddest days in my life.

On November 22, 1963, John F. Kennedy, the thirty-fifth president of the United States, was shot and killed. Something about that event motivated me to do better, to change my life. Two months later, I applied and was approved for the nursing program. Two months after that, I left for Staten Island and Willow Brook State School.

Willow Brook State School was a school for mentally challenged children. It was a God-awful place. I spent what was the most depressing year of my life there. Children were neglected and often abused by caregivers. Thankfully, I was in classes most of the time, but I did have to spend some time working on the wards.

During my year in Staten Island, I spent a lot of time with many of the African American students at Willow Brook. For the first time, at age twenty-two, I began to interact with other people of color. I was also introduced to big city life, New York City life. New York City was just a stone's throw across the Verrazano Narrows Bridge. All my Black classmates, most of whom were a bit younger than me, took me under their wing, which was good and sometimes not so good.

We spent almost every weekend in Brooklyn or the city. Coney Island became my favorite spot. My diet was usually Nathan's hotdogs, fries, and a huge beer. Other than my senior year at high school, this time was my most exciting year. It was both exciting and distracting. The distractions caused me to fall behind, and I wasn't asked to return for my second year. Soon after, I found myself back in Upstate New York. I had lost all my interest and motivation to go back to Willard. But I had not lost my desire to finish my nursing education, nor my desire to return to the big city, any big city. A year later, my wife and I moved from Ovid to Painted Post, New York. She got a job as a nurse at Corning Hospital, and I enrolled at Corning Community College in their two-year RN degree program. Soon after, my second son, Scott, was on the way.

A New Direction

When I was accepted as a nursing student at Corning Community College, they also accepted most of the credits I had earned at Willow Brook. I took on two part-time jobs while going to school full time. I even played intramural sports. It was during this time that my mother and I reunited. My mother had major back surgery and was unable to work. I went to Chicago and picked up her and Patrick and moved them in with me in Painted Post.

Five miles from Painted Post is Corning, where Corning Glassware is made. The community college was largely a commuter school attended by middle and upper-income students. About twenty-five percent of students were Black. However, there were few activities outside of intramural sports for Black and other minority students. The college had a huge spring weekend festival each May, which had little or no participation by the minority students. It was 1968, a time when the whole *Black is Beautiful* movement was beginning to gain momentum. I joined a group of students who petitioned the college to use student activities fees to provide more events and activities for minorities. The student activities department asked me to serve as student chairman of the spring weekend festival. It was surely intended to be a put-up-or-shut-up assignment. It was the first time in the college's history that an African American served as the chairman, and entertainment was a big deal.

One big reason minority students had not participated in earlier events was the lack of any R&B artists and music, which included the weekend Spring Concert Jam. I put together a committee which included some minority students, and we devised an entertainment plan. We had the biggest local and regional bands that weekend, many of them R&B bands. The headline act was Archie Bell & The Drells from Houston. The gym was sold out the night of the show. The weekend was the first financially successful weekend the college ever had. It was also the most well-attended.

As a nursing student, working in a hospital two days every week brought back bad memories of my experience at Willard and Willow Brook. I was never comfortable with bathing people, but that's what nurses do. I got on the nursing track to eventually go back to Willard as a ward supervisor, not a giver of bed baths. So, when I graduated with an A.A.S. in Nursing, I dreaded the idea of working where the majority of my day would be spent bathing and cleaning.

At that point, going back to Willard had lost its charm. I thought about what I might do with a nursing degree other than work in a hospital. This was a time when nurses began to go to anesthesiology schools to become nurse anesthetists.

I applied to several anesthesiology schools. Almost every good school had at least a two-year waiting list. I finally had my nursing degree yet was not sure what would be my next move. Before I had to decide, someone decided for me. The college staff had taken notice that I had organized and managed the first successful spring weekend. The director of student activities offered me a staff position at the college as his assistant. I would be coordinating all future spring weekend activities as well as other college programs. I did not hesitate in accepting, and my nursing career was put on hold.

Black Students Takeover Willard Straight Hall

In the fall of 1968, I began my job as student activities assistant. I developed and helped implement various activities campus-wide. It was ironic that before that next spring weekend, an event at Cornell University would change my career path again.

Cornell University was located in Ithaca, and like many other universities across America at the time, it was trying to handle massive student unrest and protests. In the spring of 1969, there was a lot of tension between the White and the emerging Black student population. This was taking place as the nation struggled with a growing civil rights movement. Cornell was just one of several hotbeds of unrest in the country.

Soon after students returned to Cornell in January 1969, there were three incidents where White males raped African American female students on campus. It was the final straw in a year-long program of harassment and intimidation heaped on Black students by White fraternities. A newly formed Black student organization, CBSU (Cornell Black Student Union), had for many months tried unsuccessfully to get more campus police protection in the North Campus section. North Campus was where most of the Black students lived. Cornell had three student union buildings. The largest was Willard Straight Hall. So large, in fact, that the building had hotel rooms where parents stayed during Parents Weekend.

April 19, 1969: the rooms were full of parents on the chilly spring morning. About a dozen Black students from CBSU stormed Willard Straight Hall, evicted the parents, and locked down the building. The takeover in the sleepy city of Ithaca became the lead story locally and nationally on newscasts and in newspapers across the nation. The takeover of Willard Straight Hall lasted three days. During those three days, James Perkins, the university's president, negotiated with leaders of the students about issues they demanded be addressed before they would leave the building. After an agreement was reached the students left on the morning of April 22, 1969.

What shocked the nation again was a photograph of the Black students leaving Willard Strait Hall armed with guns. The photographer who took the picture won a Pulitzer Prize for capturing their departure. What was omitted from the story was how the guns ended up there. Two days after the takeover, a group of White fraternity students armed themselves and began talking about going in and taking back the building. A group of Black students heard of the plan and armed themselves for protection, bringing the guns in through a back door. That, as Paul Harvey would say is: "the rest of the story" but still an untold story.

Among the items on the students' list of demands was a requirement to recruit and hire more Black staff and faculty at the university. Cornell was one of several universities nationwide that were under similar pressures. This was the backdrop when I received a call in late April from Vince Trotter, the Dean of Students at Alfred State University in New York.

Vince Trotter was looking for an assistant to help coordinate student activities. Not long before I got that call, my mother and brother moved in with me. I went to Alfred for an interview and was offered the job on the spot. I submitted my resignation at Corning and moved my family to Alfred. Just one month after taking the position, I made a decision that almost cost me the job.

Campus Unrest Shocks the Nation

Alfred State University is a small agricultural technical college that like Cornell, forty-eight miles away, was struggling with providing programs and staff to a growing African American student population. Therefore, my job involved creating, implementing, and coordinating various activities of interest to those students. I was also asked to help teach a class by one of the history professors to present and lead discussion about African American contributions to American history and related issues. So, there I was at twenty-five, sporting an incredible Afro and teaching at a university.

I had been closely following the Willard Straight Hall incident. I decided to invite three African American students, one of whom had been involved in the takeover, to come to Alfred State to talk about what happened. The auditorium I booked for the event held 350 people. The program was to start at high noon on Wednesday. It was a time when both Black students and White students were protesting against the Vietnam war, rampant racism, and social injustice. By 11:00 a.m., the auditorium was already filled, and several hundred people stood in line to get in. My boss was nervous about the event. He wanted to know if he should call campus security to fend off any potential problems. He told me in no uncertain terms that he would hold me responsible if anything went wrong. It was an incredible three-hour program that went off without incident. Trotter apologized for his concerns, and we had a great working relationship the rest of the time I worked there.

Vince Trotter had hired a young married couple as dorm supervisors. It turned out to be a big problem for the Dean. They basically suspended all rules and regulations for their dorm and let students establish their own rules. Obviously, that did not go over well with Trotter or the university. He ended up firing the couple, and I ended up moving from university housing with my family to the dorm they left in turmoil. I was tasked with bringing some order and stability to the dorm and was able to do so rather quickly. My initial plan had been to move back to my family housing unit after a new supervisor was hired. But before that happen, I got a call from Ron Loomis. Ron was the director of student unions at Cornell, with an office in Willard Straight Hall.

Cornell had been working on a five-year plan to increase Black staff and faculty. I traveled to Ithaca some weeks later and was hired. Ironically, my office there had been a hotel suite in Willard Straight Hall. All the hotel rooms had been converted to offices shortly after the unrest. That Parents Weekend was the last ever. My move to Ithaca and Cornell University was a game-changer in both my career and in my family.

Life in the Fast Lane

Before moving to Cornell, my wife and I moved our life with Terry and Scott to Alfred. Soon after our move, we began to have some issues with our marriage, which was a major part of my decision to take up residence in the dorm. Two more sons, Mark and Blake had also joined the family. When I arrived at Cornell, Sharon and I had been granted a legal separation; two years later, we divorced. I was on my own again.

In April 1971, I arrived at a much different Cornell University than the one of April two years earlier. The previous events and the subsequent fallout had dramatically changed Cornell, and I was among the fast-growing number of African American staff and faculty. As program director of university unions, I oversaw the coordination of all student activities and events that took place in all three student union buildings: including speakers, coffee house events, exhibits, meetings, movies, craft shows, dances, plays, and concerts. Soon after I took the job, I hired a staff member who worked at the American Program Bureau as a booking agent; his name was Bob Davis. I had worked with Bob in hiring speakers for a speaker's program we conducted at Willard Straight Hall.

Cornell's Barton Hall was a cavernous building on campus that was a part of the ROTC program. It could seat 50,000 people. The acoustics were horrible, but Bob and his student staff hired one of the biggest sound companies in the country to provide sound and light for concerts held there. He brought in some of the biggest acts in the county; rock, R&B, country, pop, Bob hired it all.

The Cornell Concert Commission included Bob and a group of students, who not only put on concerts for students during the school year but also put on concerts for the general population during the summer. They brought in acts like Ike and Tina Turner, Jethro Tull, The Eagles, James Taylor, Grateful Dead, Hank Williams, The Temptations, Diana Ross, etc. My office had pretty much been a one-man show when I first arrived, so I had to share Ron's secretary.

By the end of my first year, there were so many activities, programs, and events that I told Ron I needed another staff member. I eventually attended the ACUI (Association of College Unions International) conference with the hopes of hiring an assistant. I hired an energetic, young African American woman, Willda Shaw, who worked with all the other department heads in coordinating activities between buildings. It was the best hire I ever made for the unions. During those times, Cornell University had perhaps the finest student activity staff in America. Two years later, Willda and I began dating, and a year after that, we were married in a garden ceremony on campus.

The year before the wedding, one African American law student came to me with a problem that would change my life and put me on a new career path that would last twenty-eight years.

EJ Smoke

EJ Smoke Is Born

By 1973, the newly hired staff at Cornell University Unions was on a roll. We were having great success in bringing many big music stars, lecturers, and films. We were also creating programs and activities that were important to the growing African American population. In the early seventies, Cornell, like thousands of other universities, could feel the energy and awareness young Black Americans brought to their respective campuses. The city, excluding students at Cornell and Ithaca College, had a Black population of less than 6%. Many of the Black students coming to Cornell were from the New York City area.

There were a lot of things that had been a part of those student's daily lives that were missing in Ithaca. One of them was a Black radio station. In the early seventies, Black music had become "America's music" and was a driving force in the cultural awakening of Black Americans, especially those attending college. Black radio stations across America were the heart of that awareness. In Ithaca, only one radio station was playing R&B.

In May 1973, a group of communications students, most from New York City, came to me and asked if I would be their staff advisor. They had a problem. The group had organized a student activities club called *The Sounds of Blackness*. They wanted me to help them preserve a four-hour R&B music show they had on local radio station WTKO-AM. The show aired from 8:00 p.m. until 12:00 p.m. every Sunday, and they needed someone who lived in Ithaca during the summer to take over. Because all club members went home in summer, they weren't available, so I said I would do it.

I don't think I had ever been inside a radio station before then, but I went to the station to do an air check. In radio, an air check is a tape recording of how you will sound on the air. They wanted to make sure I could speak English properly! Of course, I could. The following Sunday, I went on the air hosting WTKO's Sunday night *Sounds of Blackness* as radio host—EJ Smoke. After just one night, I was hooked. From that day on, I would spend the next twenty-eight years with radio as a part of my daily life.

Broadcasting and Photography Changes Everything

It was 1974. Richard Nixon had resigned as the thirty-seventh president of the United States. There was the "rumble in the jungle" between Muhammed Ali and Joe Frazier, and everyone was watching Soul Train. We were listening to Stevie Wonder, James Brown, The Spinners, and the Jackson Five on the radio. While I continued my full-time job at Cornell, I was Ithaca's only Black DJ. EJ Smoke was jamming the hits for all those in Ithaca who loved R&B. Love was on air and in the air.

On Memorial Day weekend that year, Willda Jean Shaw and I married. It was a small ceremony with just a few friends and Patrick, who was living close by in Maryland. Willda was an only child and her father was retired Army. Her parents wanted to have a big church wedding for their only child; we really didn't want that. We had already married earlier in the year without telling her parents. Yet, we let them plan a big August wedding for us in Asbury Park, New Jersey. We took off our rings, had them cleaned and polished, and became husband and wife for a second time, and never told them about the first wedding.

By then, I had worked for almost two years at the radio station. And I loved every minute of it. EJ Smoke soon became a local celebrity after Bob Davis, my employee, hired me as the DJ at a nightclub he'd opened in downtown Ithaca called the Unicorn. (He had also given Willda away at our first wedding.) I had come to love radio. After a WTKO staff member, who had been doing sports for the station abruptly left, the station owner asked me if I would take on the sports duties. I jumped at the opportunity. The job included calling play-by-play for Ithaca high school football and basketball. Now I was really hooked.

After many long discussions with Willda, I decided to take a leave of absence from Cornell and enroll in the radio and television program at nearby Ithaca College. Ithaca College has a renowned radio & television program, one of the best in the country. They've graduated notables like Jessica Savage, the first female news anchor on network television, Emmy-award-winning sportscaster Bob Costas, and without question the most successful, Robert Iger, the current CEO of the Walt Disney empire. Ithaca College accepted all my previous credits from Corning, which enabled me to get my bachelor's degree in a year and two summers, while I continued my sports work at WTKO.

I also worked for the local cable company selling subscriptions. After joining the company, they asked me to host a local community, public affairs show titled *Black View Point*. It was a fifteen-minute weekly show with a focus on issues and topics of interest to African Americans. Most shows were taped in-studio and aired the next week. When one of my weekly guests invited me to join him on a visit to Muhammed Ali's training camp, I jumped at the chance.

We spent two days at Ali's camp in the Pennsylvanian mountains and recorded enough footage to do three, fifteen-minute shows. During the two-day taping, Ali was much like he was in public: constantly full of jokes, poems, and gags. It was an experience of a lifetime! By this time, I was beginning to have second thoughts about returning to Cornell after I graduated.

I was also becoming serious about the wonderful world of photography. I had been taking pictures all my adult life. The Finger Lakes offer incredible scenery all year round. I'd always had a camera but had never taken art seriously. That was until I took a photography course at Ithaca.

The final grade was given for your portfolio presentation. You had to shoot, develop, mat, and mount a series of your photos. I shot my portfolio in Watkins Glen State Park, which sits at the foot of Seneca Lake. It is the longest and deepest of the eleven Finger Lakes that dot central New York[1], only thirty miles from Lodi Point, invoking memories of my mother taking us to the park on summer holidays. My portfolio received an A+ and was judged best in class.

The added bonus of being selected best in class was my portfolio being displayed in the campus student union for three months. This was the beginning of my lifelong pursuit of photographic excellence. I would hardly be without a camera for the rest of my life. In the summer of 1975, I informed my boss Ron Loomis that I would not be returning to my job at Cornell.

I took a part-time sales job at WTKO in late 1975. The station put together a bicentennial sales package that included radio spots for $17.76. I sold more packages than all the other sales teams combined. Most were sold to new clients, the heartbeat of a radio station. So, the general manager offered me a full-time sales position, and six months later, I was sales manager. When the GM left a few months after, they offered me his position.

I hired a young man who had been a friend and colleague of mine at Ithaca College. His name was Gordon Thomas. He'd been my broadcast partner for Ithaca College and high school football and basketball games. Gordon informed me that Cornell University had just hired a high school coach from Hempstead, New York to be the lacrosse coach, Richie Moran. Gordon knew him and had a hunch Moran would take the already outstanding Cornell lacrosse program to another level; and that he did! WHCU-FM was a competing radio station in Ithaca that had the broadcast right to all Cornell sports. But in spring 1976, they weren't broadcasting Cornell lacrosse. Gordon asked me about meeting with the athletic director at Cornell to ask for permission to broadcast. At the time, this was Dick Schultz, who later served as the executive director of the NCAA. During our meeting with Schultz, he picked up the phone and called the GM at WHCU-FM and asked his opinion point-blank. His response was, "No one is interested in lacrosse."

One month later, Gordon and I were in the broadcast booth calling the 1976 home opener for the Cornell lacrosse team. They won the game and went undefeated, finishing the season at 18–0 and winning the NCAA National Championship. The following year, WHCU-FM called Dick Schultz to inform him that they now wanted to do the lacrosse games. He told them they could, but he was going to let us continue as well. After all, we had been there when WHCU had no interest.

The next year, the team went undefeated again at 17–0 and won a second consecutive championship, which was played at Brown University. Gordon and I arrived at the stadium early to check broadcast lines and gather roster information on Cornell's opponent, the University of Maryland. About three hours before the game, while looking down on the field, I noticed someone walking around in a gold blazer: emblematic of someone with ABC sports. After I got out my binoculars, I recognized the man as Frank Gifford.

He is a hall of fame broadcaster, but he had never broadcast or even seen a lacrosse game. So many high school teams played a practice game to give Gifford a better understanding of the rules. ABC did not broadcast the game live; instead they edited Frank's game call and played it back on ABC Wide World of Sports a week later. After just two years in radio, Gordon and I had broadcast two undefeated seasons of Cornell lacrosse and back-to-back national championships with the bigwigs. By then, we had big heads.

Farewell to New York State

My radio career and love for sports broadcasting continued at WTKO for another year. Gordon and I continued with high school football and Cornell basketball. Our favorite basketball road trips were the back-to-back stops: one night at Princeton and then the second at world-famous Palestra in the city of brotherly love, Philadelphia. We knew we were in the big leagues when one time we walked into those arenas an hour before broadcast time. Gordon was sporting a navy blazer and tan bell-bottoms, while I wore a gold Nehru jacket with navy bell-bottoms. We were clean, and all eyes were on us as we entered the arena.

We had some great times with road broadcasting events. As I look back on those times, I remember them as some of the most enjoyable of life. I began thinking about how someday I might get the chance to broadcast collegiate or even professional sports somewhere in a big city. Gordon and I talked a lot about how we would one day be wearing *the gold blazer*. I also thought about how maybe one day my hometown team would win an NBA championship, or a World Series, or a Super Bowl. What I didn't know was that forty-three years later, the first of those three dreams would come true. Life was good in small Ithaca. My job as WTKO's GM continued as the station's revenue and audience ratings grew.

It all changed in 1979 when I got a call from a headhunter who worked for Paul Nuehoff. Paul was the owner of two radio stations in Cleveland, Ohio. The radio stations were WGCL-FM and WERE-AM, a rock station and the leading news/talk station in Cleveland. The headhunter told me that Paul was looking for a sales manager for WERE-AM, and he wanted to talk to me about the position. After the initial phone interview, Paul flew me to Cleveland for a face-to-face. One week later, he offered me the job. Willda and I hastily said our goodbyes to friends and family and moved to Cleveland, which held a tie to the past.

My mother and father had divorced when I was ten years old and Norma nine. Not having a father and growing up as a Black male in a small White town had never been an issue for me. My mother played both roles. Moving forward in life and working at Alfred State, I'd become friends with two colleagues as all three of us were big-time football fans. Out of the blue, I called my mother who had moved to Silver Springs, Maryland by then and asked her if she knew where my father lived. She said she didn't, but she would try to find out. She found out from a family member that he lived in Cleveland. After, I got a Cleveland phone directory and began to randomly call Ernest Jacksons in Cleveland.

I had gotten about halfway through when I found him. He was happy to hear from me. He had remarried and had two sons with his new wife. I told him my two friends and I had been planning a trip to a Cleveland Browns game. He was excited to see me. We drove to Cleveland, and I had the chance to see my father for the first time since we'd departed some thirty years earlier. He was indeed happy to see me, and we spent a long weekend with him and his family. We stayed in touch the next five years, but I lost track of him in 1979 when he moved to another area of Cleveland.

Shortly after Willda and I got settled in, I began the process of locating my father all over again. Using the same method, I found him. The first question he asked me was whether I was still in Ithaca. I told him I was not, and I had moved to Cleveland. We renewed our relationship for the short time I was there.

Just one year after I arrived in Cleveland, Paul Neuhoff left the stations. Paul and I had a great working relationship, and when he departed, I wasn't sure I wanted to continue work under new ownership. When I called Paul to discuss this, he told me to hold tight; he was working on an opportunity he wanted me to be a part of. Six months later, he told me he had formed a minority broadcast company with George Forbes, the president of the Cleveland City Council. He and George were considering buying two stations near Charleston. He asked me to fly to Charleston and spend a few days to assess the opportunity.

The two radio stations were WDWQ-FM and WQIZ-AM; both licensed to St George, South Carolina, a small town about forty miles north of Charleston. The radio stations had some serious technical issues, and as a result, you could not hear either of them in most of Charleston. WDWQ-FM was an R&B station and WQIZ-AM a gospel station. Paul planned to switch the format on WDWQ-FM from R&B to top forty.

There was no real top forty station in Charleston, and he thought that if we relocated the radio tower thirty miles closer to Charleston, it would put out a stronger signal. I told him I thought the plan was sound, and I asked what he needed of me. He wanted me to move to Charleston to take a position as the VP & GM over the stations. Neither he nor George wanted to move there. So, after just eighteen months in Cleveland, I was off to my third radio job. I was now separated for the third time from my father, and this time would be the last. Two years after I arrived in South Carolina, my father died. I often wondered how I ended up in Cleveland for just eighteen months. It would be the shortest stay in my twenty-eight-year career. I believe it happened to give me a chance to renew my relationship with my father before he died.

Opportunity in South Carolina

The move to Charleston was the first time Willda or I lived in the deep south. Charleston was a beautiful antebellum city nestled in a harbor. For the first time, we were living where many of the attitudes and practices had not changed since the enactment of Jim Crow. I got my first taste of that very early. The two stations Paul and George purchased were licensed to St. George, and I did not want to live there, so we bought a house in Charleston, which meant about an hour drive one-way. The stations were not productive or profitable, and the physical plant was rundown. I hadn't been on the job for more than a week when I stepped on a rusty nail leaving the station. I didn't want to drive all the way back to Charleston to have it checked out, so I went to the local doctor's office.

It was a small place with two waiting rooms. It was obvious to me as soon as I walked in that the waiting rooms were for different clients. In one waiting room, all the patients were Black, and in the other, everyone was White. There were no signs to tell you which was which, but the local people knew. It was 1981 in the deep south. It was a rude awakening to the way things were even after Jim Crow was rumored to have left America.

It took me a few months to begin to sort out the most troublesome problems at the radio station. One problem I wrestled with was how long to continue the R&B format on WQIZ-FM. The first challenge I tackled was to find totally new staff. The previous staff wouldn't have been able to execute the top forty format, so I hired two key people.

36   Health, Heart, and Pocketbook

One was Ron Pinkney, a.k.a. Ron Kay, an eventual lifelong friend. Ron had some valuable experience as a DJ at one of the gospel stations in Charleston. His role was to hold up the revenue because we knew when we switched, we would lose most, if not all revenue on the station.

The original plan was to hold off on a format switch until I found a piece of land closer to Charleston to put a tower and antenna. I decided not to wait, and I changed the format and call letters on WQIZ-FM to WDWQ-FM. This was how radio station Q-107 was born. I hired another local DJ who had experience doing top forty radio. Within six months, Q-107 was pumping out hits from Hall & Oats, Blondie, ABBA, and the Air Supply; The Temptations, Four Tops, and the OJay's were gone. Although the station could still not be heard in the entire city, the new format was an immediate success. The Arbitron (the company that measures radio audience) ratings went through the roof. Right out of the shoot, Q-107 went from a 1.9 rating to a 9.1. Success, however, brought challenges.

When I switched the format, the goal was to attract advertisers who never had a need or a desire to advertise on the little R&B station. Our hope was to draw in car dealers, banks, soft drink companies, and furniture stores. Most of the businesses on WQIZ-FM had been nightclubs and mom-and-pop stores. When the station climbed to 9.1, some of the White-owned stations filed a petition with the FCC (Federal Communication Commission) to deny our application to move our radio antenna. What should have taken three or four months took nearly two years.

Meanwhile, despite a poor signal, the ratings and the revenue grew. The ultimate game changer that got the FCC application approved was my chance meeting with Pluria Marshall. Sr. Pluria was the head of the National Black Media Coalition (NBMC), a watchdog organization in Washington, D.C., whose goal was to promote and enhance minority ownership of radio and television.

Pluria was a bulldog and then some. He was well-respected in the communication circles in Washington and had the ear of the FCC chairman. I went to Washington and met with Pluria to ask for his support. He went straight to the FCC and argued that because our company was minority-owned, we were entitled under FCC mandate to receive expedited treatment for our application. After a few meetings with key officials and because of Pluria's no-holds-barred approach, we finally got approval. Pluria and I became good friends, and our paths crossed a number of times.

Paul Neuhoff had said once we were successful in building the two radio stations, he wanted me to do the same thing with two properties in Sacramento. The two and a half years commuting eighty miles roundtrip every day, as well as the battle with the White broadcasters took a toll on me. So, when I got a call from Earnest James, about a job in Memphis, I was ready to listen. After several conversations and a face-to-face interview, I resigned from my position at Q-107 and WQIZ-AM and accepted the VP & GM position at WDIA-AM. That move would launch my broadcast career on a rocket ride to success.

Radio Majic

America's Oldest Black Radio Station

In October 1983, Ernest James brought me to Memphis to serve the oldest Black formatted radio station in America. WDIA went on the air in 1947, offering a variety of music, mostly country. Its original owners, John Pepper and Bert Ferguson, realized early on that the station's format wasn't going to be successful. It was just like everything else on the radio dial in Memphis. WDIA was further handicapped by being on the AM band at a time when FM ruled. Ferguson realized there was one format with a potential listening audience that was not being served by Memphis radio. That prompted Ferguson to change WDIA to an all-Black formatted station, and he hired the first Black disk jockey ever in the South. He was Nat D. Williams, who'd been a syndicated columnist and high school teacher.

It was one of the very first radio programs in the U.S. to appeal to Black listeners. Soon after the switch, WDIA became the number two most listened-to radio station in Memphis. It wasn't long before the station became the city's top station. In 1954, WDIA was approved to increase its power from 250 watts to 5,000 watts and moved from 740 on the radio dial to 1070. Its powerful signal reached the Mississippi Delta's dense African American population and was heard from the Missouri border to the Gulf. WDIA reached 10% of the Black population in the U.S. There's a long list of historic air legends at WDIA. But, the greatest of them all was A.C. "Mohan" Williams.

In 1954, Williams, who was a disc jockey, created the WDIA Goodwill Fund. In those early years, the fund provided transportation to schools for disabled Black children. Later, it expanded to include college scholarships, establish boys' clubs, provide for little league baseball teams, and supply funds to start a community housing project called The Goodwill Homes. Many music legends got their start working at WDIA, including B.B. King and Rufus Thomas.

B.B. King had a daily 15-minute show promoting a patent medicine called Pep-It-Kong, and later, Lucky Strike cigarettes became the first national advertiser for the station. Throughout the early years, Bert Ferguson, a White man, served as its GM. All station management was White. In 1972, Charles "Chuck" Scruggs became its first Black GM. He served in that position for eleven years when in 1983 I became the second African American and third GM in the station's thirty-six-year history. There is little debate that WDIA was the most community service-driven radio station in the history of broadcasting. It was both a challenge and an honor to have served seven years there. My management team, my support team, and my air personalities were involved in an incredible array of community service efforts.

Mound Bayou was the background for one of these efforts. A city in Mississippi and about a ninety-minute drive from Memphis, Mound Bayou is one of, if not, the oldest Black cities in America. Former slaves freed by Jefferson Davis founded it in 1887. Its 98.6%

Black population makes it one of the highest percentage Black cities in America. In 1980, Ernestine Walker, a White woman on her way to Memphis, fell into an open manhole on city property. She sued the city and in 1983 received a judgment of $59,000, which the city didn't have. The week before Easter, the city was about to go bankrupt. The courts froze the cities assets and were about to shut off electrical power to city hall when WDIA stepped up.

Bill Atkins, a news anchor at WDIA, invited Earl Lucas, the mayor of Mound Bayou, to appear on his *Sunday Morning Live* show. After Lucas told his story, people began to line up at the front door of the radio station to offer donations. Carl Conner, the station's program director, had to call in staff on a Sunday to open the doors and let donors in. For the next seven days, the station became a donation center as the people offered nickels, dimes, and dollars. Midweek, a blind man came and said he wanted to donate money. When he was asked how much, he took all the money he had out of his pocket and asked, "How much do I have?" The following Sunday on Easter, the radio station took everything donated that week and presented it to Mayor Earl Lucas.

Early that morning, an approximately 800-car caravan was escorted by Tennessee State Police from the radio station to the Mississippi state line and then by Mississippi State Police to Mound Bayou. Mound Bayou's population was 2,900 people. But at city hall, a crowd near 15,000 saw Bill Atkins present a check for $120,000 to Earl Lucas. WDIA over the next several weeks raised another $15,000 to a total of $135,000. The story got national attention and became a segment on *60 Minutes* a few months later.

Ronald Ward roused another effort from WDIA. In 1985, seventy-six-year-old Lois Townsend, her seventy-seven-year-old sister, Aubrey Townsend, and their 12-year-old great-grandnephew were found slain in what was purported to be a drug house in West Memphis, Arkansas. It was a city just across the Mississippi River from Memphis. A day after the murders, fifteen-year-old Ronald Ward, an African American being raised by an elderly grandmother, was arrested outside his school when he was found wandering around school grounds covered in blood.

The blood matched the blood type of at least two of the victims. Ward was indicted, tried, and found guilty by an all-White jury after just fifteen minutes of deliberation. He was sentenced to die one year later. At fifteen, Ward became the youngest person in the U.S. on death row. In my job, I had a propensity for doing editorials on the radio. Most often, they were about issues affecting the Black community in Memphis. I went on the air the day after Ward's verdict with an editorial asking WDIA listeners to write letters and sign petitions to have Ronald Ward's trial and conviction investigated. In a little over two weeks, we were able to gather over 150,000 signatures.

At the same time, a young ambitious democrat served as the governor of Arkansas. His name was William Jefferson Clinton. There were rumors that he was interested in running for president. Knowing that, we packed up the 150,000 petitions and letters in two WDIA vans and deliver them to Bill Clinton at the capitol in Little Rock, Arkansas. I got an appointment to see Clinton through his chief of staff.

During the petition campaign, I had received some pretty nasty letters from people who were on the opposite side of the issue. As a result and as a precaution, our vans were escorted to the Arkansas state line by Tennessee State Police. After we crossed the bridge over the Mississippi River into Arkansas, we were pulled over by two Arkansas state police cars. When I politely inquired as to why, one of the officers told us that they would escort us to the State Capitol. When we arrived, there was a large contingent of television reporters waiting at the capitol steps. We met for about a half-hour with then-Governor Clinton, and he accepted all the mailbags with the 150,000 signatures. Almost a year later, because of Clinton's intervention, Ronald Ward was given a new trial. He was tried, this time by a jury of his peers, and once again found guilty; however, his sentence was changed from the death penalty to life in prison without parole.

I always thought young Ronald Ward got caught up in a drug deal gone bad and was probably in that house at some point, but I don't believe he had anything to do with their deaths. Ward got his G.E.D. and earned some college credits while in prison. He died on June 29, 2007, in a prison and maintained his innocence up until he died.

There were so many more incredible community projects I was involved in at WDIA. We sold gasoline to our listeners for 10.7 cents per gallon if they had a WDIA bumper sticker on their car. We created a street carnival in Tom Lee Park on the river that featured artists like The O'Jays, Harold Melvin and The Blue Notes, The Whispers, and others. The two-day festival had been free to everyone. We started an annual barbecue contest called the Bobby O'Jays "I love my Job Barbecue Cooking Contest" since Bobby was the morning air personality and program director for the station. We continued to support many of the institutions that WDIA founded and donated to in its early days.

When I arrived in Memphis, despite its history and tradition, WDIA was struggling like all AM radio stations at the time. The challenge was how to grow revenue and attract more listeners on an AM station. There were two major competitors in the market: WLOK, a gospel station, and WHRK a powerhouse R&B station. WHRK was the number-one Black formatted station with 6.8 shares of the Memphis market. WDIA was number two among Black stations with a 4.3 share. I stole a dynamic Janet Armstead from WLOK to be my sales manager. Almost overnight, she changed the entire sales staff, and we saw immediate double-digit revenue growth. I'd hired Bobby O'Jay as the program director to take the station back to its roots and heritage with a musical format mixed with talk. We soon saw the listening audience grow.

During that time, WDIA was owned by US Radio, a minority-owned broadcast company in Philadelphia. In 1985, Adams Communication purchased WDIA-AM and WHRK-FM and moved them together in studios in downtown Memphis. When the sale was announced, the speculation in the market was that Don Boyles, a White man and the GM at WHRK, would get the job for both radio stations. Matt Mills was the CEO of Adams Communication, and we had several meetings during the wait for the FCC to approve the sale. It took only three months to get that approval, and the day the sale was final, Matt called to tell me he was making me the VP & GM for both stations. Also, that year, my wife, Willda gave birth to our first and only son together, Matthew William Jackson.

That same year, I made a market visit to our national sales company in New York City. By this time, my mother had moved back to Ithaca. I decided at the end of my two-day visit that I would surprise her. She surprised me. When I got to Ithaca, I found her sick in bed with pneumonia. I had been trying to get her out of Ithaca for some years because Ithaca has such long and harsh winters. I went back two months later and moved her to Memphis where she lived with Wild and me.

My wife Willda is an only child, and she desperately wanted children. She had some medical issues that caused her to be unable to carry a fetus to full-term. As a result, she suffered several miscarriages during our first ten years of marriage. She'd been pregnant when my mother moved in with us that year. For the first time since we'd been married, she conceived and carried a fetus to seven and a half months. That was four months longer than any other pregnancy. To this day, we both believe it was the presence of Rosie Mae Jackson that enabled us to have Matthew in our lives.

During this time, I was able to fulfill a promise I'd made to my mother as a youngster. From my earliest memories of living in Ovid, my mother had always said someday before she died, she wanted to go to Hawaii. November 13, on her seventy-fifth birthday, I gave her a book with pictures of Hawaii; inside the book were also airline tickets for the family. She cried for two days! She opened the book every day until we left, and every day she cried. I will never forget the afternoon we landed in Hawaii. As soon as we left baggage claim and stepped out of the airport, she started to cry and continued all the way to our hotel.

The good year continued at the new radio station combo, WDIA-AM/WHRK-FM, which took off like a rocket in both audience and revenue growth. We now had a powerful combo that reached African Americans from eighteen years old to eighty. When the stations had been competitors, the combined audience share for the two stations was 11.1. One year after the merger, WHRK-FM had a 12.4 audience share, and AM had a 7.2 audience share for a combined 19.6. Matt Mills later called to tell me Adams Communication, who had bought WDIA and WHRK for $4,000,000, was selling the stations back to US Radio for $14,000,000.

US Radio was owned by Ragan Henry, a Philadelphia attorney who owned fifteen other stations. He'd told me one day he would want to own a radio station in his hometown and that I would have the chance to be the GM when that happened. The plan was still on the table in 1989 when Ragan asked me to move to Norfolk, Virginia before Philadelphia and run two stations he had purchased there. So, in October, I said farewell to the dedicated and compassionate group of broadcast professionals I worked with at WDIA-AM.

My time at WDIA was, without question, a time that molded the rest of my radio career, and everything I did in radio after. The experience was the building block for all the success I had for the next twenty years of my career. But, it wasn't without trying times.

Martin Luther King Jr. had given his life for the civil rights movement in America: assassinated in downtown Memphis. The assassination suspended a cloud over Memphis; it has never gone away. The White power brokers there hold a grip on African Americans unlike any other place in America. It would take me another ten pages to reconstruct that history. There has been some movement toward more social and economic justice and equality, but on the whole, most people of color hang on the lowest rung of the ladder.

Broken Radio Stations in Norfolk Virginia

Norfolk is a waterfront city in southeastern Virginia: population of about 250,000. Norfolk was not on the list of places I wanted to move to. I went because I trusted in Ragan's promise to get me to Philadelphia someday.

The two stations there were WOWI-FM and WBSK-AM. Ragan bought them from Bishop A.D. Willis, who also owned two churches and a bank. Bishop Willis owned three radio stations in Norfolk, but he kept one for himself. By the time I moved to Norfolk, my reputation in the broadcast industry was growing as someone who fixed broken stations. I turned marginal stations into winners and rebuilt losing ones into profit centers. The two radio stations Ragan purchased in Norfolk were broken, big time. Bishop Willis kept the building his stations were in. Without a building for our stations, I ended up housed in his building. This required me to build a facility for the two stations I was to manage.

When I made a trip to Norfolk for an initial site visit, I discovered that the radio money was mixed in with the Bishop's church and bank money. It was nearly impossible to know which belonged to us. When I went to Norfolk, I left my family in Memphis since I knew it would be a full-time job and then some. I spent six months merely sorting through financial records. In the end, we settled on an amount that everyone agreed probably wasn't accurate.

WOWI-FM was R&B while WBSK-AM was traditional gospel. The African Americans were nearly 50% of the area's population. WOWI was number one among Black listeners and number seven among all listeners. I replaced most of the staff members on both stations and hired totally new management. We put the station back on the right track musically and introduced Norfolk to many of the community events and promotions I'd created in Memphis. It worked. In just over a year, WOWI continued its lead with Black listeners and became the number one station among all listeners, climbing from 7.1 ratings to 13.2.

My first month, I spent my weekends looking for a house for my family. I was not excited about the prospect of living in Norfolk, so I concentrated my house hunting efforts in and around Virginia Beach. On a Saturday morning walk, looking at houses, I ran into a fellow named, Mel Collins. He lived in the neighborhood, so we chatted awhile, and he invited me to lunch at his place. Mel Collins would become a lifelong friend and the source of an addiction that my five-year-old son would contract: the North Carolina Tar Heels. Mel's son was about the same age as Matthew, and his son and he were die-hard Tar Heel fans. Nearly twenty years later, we would find ourselves together with our sons in San Antonio. The Tar Heels had made it to the Final Four, which is when I'd run into my previous opponent, coach Jim Boeheim.

Toward the end of my first year in Norfolk, I got a call which initiated a conversation that would eventually lead to the sixth and final stop of my broadcast career. The call came from Norman Feuer, a president of the radio division at Viacom. I had known Norman when I was in Memphis since Viacom had owned WDIA for a short period. He called me about a job that was open at KMJQ-FM and KYOK-AM in Houston. The station's owner, John Lynch Sr., owned seven other radio stations across the country. He had been an offensive lineman for the Pittsburgh Steelers in their heyday. KMJQ, known as Majic102, was the number one urban contemporary station in Houston. It had fallen on hard times because a rival had changed formats from top forty to hip hop and R&B. That station, KBXX (The BOXX), was in a war with Majic102, and they were winning.

Norman thought it was the ideal career opportunity for me in the fourth-largest city and one of the top ten radio markets in America. My family had only been in Virginia five months, and I had been at WOWI/WBSK for less than a year. I told Norm my work wasn't finished in Norfolk, and I needed to stay for the time being.

Majicman and a Photography Career Merge

Norman Feuer eventually called me again. John Lynch hadn't been able to find the person he needed. Norm let me know John wanted to talk to me. I had done all I could do in Norfolk. WOWI/WBSK were well-positioned as the leading radio combo in Norfolk. The stations were running like a well-oiled machine; revenues were still growing, the audience listening, and the sales staff was in great shape. It looked like Ragan's plan to buy a station in Philadelphia was going to be on hold for some time, and I didn't see any upside for me in Norfolk. So, I decided to talk to John Lynch.

John Lynch was the CEO of Noble Broadcasting, which owned radio stations in Houston, St. Louis, San Diego, and Denver. Majic102 had a legacy in Houston and a strong commitment to the Black community. John also owned KYOK-AM in Houston, a station that had provided news and information to Houstonian African Americans. (It had taken a lead role in the integration of a Houston Walgreen's during the civil rights movement.) Majic102 had been the cash cow for the Noble company. But in the early 90s, KBXX challenged and took Majic102's number-one rank among Black adults from 18–54.

The war for revenue and ratings got nasty. The longtime GM at Majic 102 had fallen ill shortly after the war began and was out on medical leave. John needed a new general. Other than a very brief stint in Cleveland, my career had been in small market cities. However, I was headed to the top ten radio market. On the plane ride to Houston for the interview, I thought about what it might be like to finally have a childhood dream come true.

I spent two days touring Houston and listening to Majic 102 and KBXX in my hotel room. It was quickly apparent Majic 102 had lost its direction and focus. The station had started to mix a lot of hip hop into the music rotation. That chased away the station's core audience: adults 25–54. They'd also changed the station's brand from Majic 102 to 102 Jamz.

The first question John asked me when the interview began was, "What do you think about the station?" I said: "The bad news is your station is broken. The good news is I can fix it." Three hours later, John offered me the job. He wanted me to stop the bleeding right away, but I insisted on settling things in Norfolk. I'd had a great run there.

My family and I enjoyed the Virginia Beach area, and it was during my time there that I escalated my love affair with photography. While in Norfolk, I met a professor at Norfolk State University who moved my photography interest and skills to the next level. The professor introduced me to a film I had never heard of: Fuji Velia.

Velia was a slide film that had tremendous color balance and enhanced saturation. My photography prints improved by leaps and bounds. I had been shooting with Kodak Kodachrome. Once I started shooting with Velvia, I never shot another roll of Kodak. Years later, I ditched film to go digital.

One of the great things we enjoyed while in Virginia was traveling the Blue Ridge Mountain Parkway. I had bought an RV in Memphis, and I spent the summers with my family along Blue Ridge and in Smokey Mountain National Park, camping and taking photos. It was here that I began my quest to shoot and promote America's magnificent National Parks.

The Majic Is Back

When I landed in Houston, my first thought was I'd landed the job of a lifetime. My broadcast career had taken me to five different cities, managing ten radio stations. In sixteen years, I'd never been fired, and in the broadcast industry, this was a rare feat. John's offer to come to Houston even included tickets to both the major league basketball and baseball teams. I had a clause in my contract that would pay me a $150,000 bonus if I got the profit up $4,000,000 annually.

My first opportunity to see the financials came soon after I arrived. I discovered that the cash flow was down $2,000,000. At some point before the war, Majic102 was generating $24,000,000 annually. By the time I arrived, it had dropped to $15,000,000. Part of the reason I had been successful was I learned early that the key wasn't about how good I was but how good my management team was. Every time, the first thing I did was to interview every single employee at a station. I saved the department heads for last to learn how the second-level employees felt about their bosses. It made my job easier when it was time to evaluate managers. By the time I had finished, I knew what the game plan needed to be to turn things around. After meeting with the management team at Majic102, it was clear I needed to make some changes.

Those changes made were not so much because the managers did a bad job, but because I needed people with different skill sets. The three most important things in radio growth are sales, programming, and promotions. The sales folks stay on the ground, in front of advertisers every day, selling radio ads and sponsorship packages. Despite the revenue decline, I felt that the sales team and management staff were strong, which is good because changing them is absolutely the toughest.

The station had chased away a lot of adults 25–54, while BOXX took much of the adults 18–34. In my interview, I reminded John that you can't be all things to all people. Majic 102 needed to get back to its roots: R&B for 25–54: the demographic big advertisers want and need. The BOXX did well marketing to teens and young adults, but the real money was with banks, grocery stores, furniture stores, and automobile dealers. Majic 102's lifeblood. After my assessment of the staff was complete, I dropped the 102 Jamz brand. The new station brand would be, "The Majic is back."

I knew I needed someone leading the programming department, so I brought in a magic maker, Carl Conner, who'd been the program director at WDIA. Next was the promotion department, the heartbeat of community connection. It is the face of what you look like in the streets with setting up remote broadcast, coordinating DJ appearances, and managing the community events. They are the frontline soldiers. So, I brought back someone who had been at the station for several years as promotions director. Sharp and honest, Chili McCraven knew where all the bodies were buried. She was my right hand and left hand as my executive secretary until I moved her to the business office.

It is essential to hire great people, who have passion and are reliable and honest. Wherever I was, I always tried to create a work atmosphere where all employees and managers felt like they could make mistakes without fear of punishment or retaliation. If you can do that, people feel they never have to cover up mistakes. I also made sure I could do anything and everything so I never expected anyone to do something that I couldn't. When I moved Chili to executive secretary, many at the station told me to talk with Bobrie Jefferson. She'd also been the promotions director previously and gone to Fox Television. I invited her to lunch, and after twenty minutes, I knew she could lead the street team and the soldiers on the frontline. I made her an offer, and she accepted. The response to "The Majic is back" was incredible, to say the least. Bobrie and her team were the reason for much of the early success.

I also felt strongly about the sales department. I felt confident Aldie Beard, who'd been leading a strong veteran sales team for several years was a good fit. The team was all on board with the new direction and was getting prepared to present a new sales and marketing plan. After two months, Aldie Beard walked into my office with a letter from a local Attorney; the contents of which would consume almost every minute of my workday for months.

One Childhood Dream Comes True

Majic102's staff developed a new sense of pride and enthusiasm when we embarked on the campaign to bring the Majic back. New management was in place, the promotions team was in the street fighting hand-to-hand combat, and the entire station staff was energized.

Late one afternoon, Aldie Beard brought me a letter signed by several local nightclub owners, alleging that Jimmy Olsen, one of the station's most popular DJs, was involved in plugola and payola. Jimmy was one who'd been hired when Majic102 changed to 102 Jamz and had been working for The BOXX previously.

Plugola and payola have a long history in the annals of radio. The first U.S. radio stations appeared in the early 1920s, serving as a medium to broadcast news and information.[1] It quickly became clear that it could be a powerful way to advertise products and services. John R. Brinkley, a fake doctor and con artist, claimed that his treatment using goat testicles would cure male impotence and many other diseases and ailments.[2] After touring a local radio station, Brinkley got the idea to build a station to promote his cure. He made millions.

In 1923, he built a station, KFKB just outside St Louis, Missouri. At that time, no real regulatory agency oversaw radio for business.

In 1927, the Federal Radio Commission was formed but had little success in trying to regulate this growing new business.[3] The government realized that there needed to be stronger regulations on the rapidly growing industry. After complaints and lawsuits, Brinkley lost his "medical" business and radio station license in 1930.[4] Four years later, Congress passed the Telecommunications Act of 1934 and installed a new agency: the Federal Communication Commission or FCC.[5]

The FCC still enforces many rules and regulations. Most of those restrictions stood the test of time. Few changes were made to the Telecommunications Act until 1996, which President Bill Clinton signed into law.[6] After a congressional investigation, the FCC amended its rules and regulations to discourage payola and plugola. The amendment provided for huge monetary fines and possible loss of license for such violations. Plugola is when a business endorses a product or service on radio or television for personal gain.[7] Payola is when a radio station accepts payment for playing songs.[8] Both come with hefty fines if employees do either.

The nightclub owners' letter alleged Jimmy Olsen had accepted cash to bring entertainers to their respective clubs. In addition, they claimed Olsen took money for promoting their appearances at the clubs on his radio show. Because no advertising money had been spent from the station to promote the appearances, it was clearly plugola.

I immediately informed John Lynch that we had a potentially serious problem on our hands, but I had a plan. Some of my management team confirmed that they suspected Olsen had been taking money. Before I confronted him with my suspicions, I decided to talk with each of the club owners who had signed the letters. They were cautious about how much they told me because they had some legal jeopardy as well for paying Olsen. The whole matter was complicated and required me to move assiduously, and it didn't help that Olsen's dad was a local attorney with some political clout.

When I confronted Olsen, he denied everything. I suspended him with pay until an investigation could be completed. I spent several months working with a corporate attorney and a local attorney, and it became clear Olsen was guilty. Before I decided what to do with him, he turned in his resignation, and guess what? He was immediately hired back by The BOXX. With Olsen gone, I returned my undivided attention back to the radio war at hand.

It was shortly after that one of those childhood dreams was fulfilled. That dream where my hometown basketball team would win an NBA Championship. My son who was then six years old was an avid sports fan like his father, and at Magic 102, we had season tickets to the Houston Rockets. Matthew and I attended many of the Rockets' home games during 1993–1994. The Rockets went 17–1 in their first eighteen games that year and went on to win a franchise record of fifty-eight games. After being down 3–2 against the Knicks, the Rockets won game six and seven at home, winning the NBA Championship. The dream's fulfillment was made even sweeter with Matthew sitting next to me as we celebrated the first-ever NBA title for the Rockets. It was that night we heard the Rocket's Head coach, Rudy Tomjanovich say, "Don't ever underestimate the heart of a champion."

Three months later, John Lynch called me with news that would change our war, and in a way, make us champions.

The Houston Radio War Ends

Some readers may have noticed many radio stations call letters start with K and others with W. Here is why. After the FCC was established, it realized it had to find a way to identify the vast number of stations. They decided to have all call signs for radio stations west of the Mississippi River start with the letter K, and for all stations east of the Mississippi to begin with the letter W.

The Majic102/KBXX combo continued its dominance, and it looked like I would get that $150,000 bonus. So, it wasn't a complete surprise when John said he was working on a deal with Clear Channel Radio to put together Majic102 and The BOXX. If that acquisition were completed, the two stations would go from competitors to family. The war would be over. John assured me I would be a part of the new company's management team. After all, I had brought Majic102 back from the dead.

Three months later, John made a visit to the station to tell me that the joint-venture company had not materialized, and he was selling the station to Clear Channel. Clear Channel would buy The BOXX and Majic102; they would be the sole owner for $75,000,000.

The name Clear Channel had come from the early days of radio. A clear-channel station was an AM station that had the highest protection of interference from others, especially at night. The first broadcast stations could be heard for hundreds of miles across the country on fifty-two different frequencies. Most were licensed to large cities. Later more and more owners built radio stations intended to serve local communities. The Federal Radio Commission wanted to allow for local stations, but also wanted to protect the nation's original clear channels.[9] So, they required the new local stations to cut their power at night if they were on the same frequency as one of the clear channels. That way the local station would not interfere with clear channel broadcasts. Those rules were in place until 1980 when the FCC voted to limit the protection for all clear-channel stations to a 750-mile radius from its transmitter. That meant that stations outside the area of protection were no longer required to sign off after sunset. Clear Channel symbolized that protection and transformation.

They purchased their first radio station in 1972 with CEO Lowery Mays. Lowery had been a radio station broker. As a family-owned-and-operated company, Clear Channel had forty-three stations when they filed for ownership of Majic102 and KBXX. Two years earlier, the FCC had relaxed radio ownership rules to allow companies to own more than two radio stations in a single market. Before, a company could own only one AM, one FM, and one television station in a single market; and seven AM, FM, and television stations nationwide.

Majic102 and the BOXX would be the forty-fourth and forty-fifth radio stations owned by Clear Channel. Two years later, they had two hundred radio and television stations in the U.S.

During my three years at Majic102, the radio station enjoyed tremendous support from the Black community for all the great community service projects and events we held. Many of the political, business, and religious leaders in the community made it known to Clear Channel that they wanted me to continue as the head of the new station combo. Clear Channel told those community leaders that Ernie Jackson would be running everything when the combo got FCC approval. The BOXX had its own general manager, so it had been unclear officially who would lead.

It took almost a year for the FCC to approve the sale out of fear that Clear Channel might control too much revenue and program content in a single market. When the approval came, Clear Channel announced that they would have two GMs. Many community leaders were upset with this choice, and some began a campaign to try to hold Clear Channel to its promise.

Clear Channel made the right decision, and I agreed with it. Majic102 and The BOXX had been dog-eat-dog competitors. To ask the two stations to move into a single facility, and become family overnight, could be a long and difficult task. The cultures were totally opposite of one another. Late in 1995, the staff and management of

KBXX moved into the offices of Majic102 to coexist as a family. There were some trying times in those first few months, but the general manager of KBXX and I worked together to overcome most of those.

A year and a half later, the KBXX GM left to take a position as the manager of another Clear Channel station. Once I became manager for both stations, the new combo took off like a rocket. The plan was simple. KBXX was the dominant radio station in Houston among African Americans 18–34. Majic102 was the same among African Americans 25–54, so we drew a line in the sand. That line required KBXX to target their age group and Majic102 to focus on theirs. No rap on Majic102, and no adult R&B on KBXX. With that as the strategy, advertisers could reach African American listeners from 18–64. And it worked. Advertising revenue shot through the roof. Audience listening shot through the roof, and the value of the new combo shot through the roof.

Houston Radio Makes History

By the second year of the merger, the Houston Urban Contemporary combo was on a roll. In early radio, before the ownership rules changed, profit margins were expected to be in the thirty-five to forty percent range. During most of my radio career, owners would have been pleased with forty percent margins. So, it was a shock to me and my entire team when we learned that Clear Channel wanted fifty percent. At the time, it seemed impossible, and my staff thought the company had lost its mind. There was a consensus among all the Clear Channel station GMs that the goal was not realistic.

One year later, we ended up with a profit margin of fifty-eight percent. We were the company darlings. I remember CEO Mays telling me that the other radio managers didn't like us because when they went for the San Antonio budget meeting with fifty percent margins as a goal, they were asked: "Can't you do better?" Two major factors contributed to our success. The first was our ability to continually raise our advertising rates. Advertisers had to buy our combo if they were interested in reaching African Americans of all ages.

The second factor was our commitment to community service programs and events. Black radio stations had served as forces for news and the exchange of information. In fact, the Black station had always been the second most powerful and influential force in the Black community; second only to the Black church.

During my first five years in Houston, we created much goodwill and respect from the Black community and won national recognition as one of the top Urban Contemporary radio stations in the nation. I drew on all my community service experience from other radio stations, starting with WDIA. From Memphis, all around, and to Houston, the lists of historic promotions were endless. But, I had my favorites.

I love My Job Barbecue Contest

Memphis is the barbecue capital of the world. People argue and fight to extremes about who cooks the best barbecue in the city. So, we'd seized on that Memphis fervor and created the *Bobby OJay: I Love My Job Barbecue Contest*. I brought the idea to Houston, and in 1996, we conducted our first Majic102 *I Love My Job Barbecue Contest*. The idea was that co-workers, families, church groups, and others got together on a Saturday and competed in barbeque. The first year, the contest was held in a small parking lot next to the radio station. Less than twenty contestants came to spend the day cooking, drinking, listening to music, and lying about how good their barbecue was. Winners received a $1000-prize, a trophy, and bragging rights for a year.

By the fourth year, we had to move the contest to a large park where we had over fifty contestants after we turned away hundreds from lack of space. We had politicians, pastors, businessmen, celebrities, and station listeners serving as judges. And of course, we sold sponsorships to advertisers.

Majic102 Gas Sale

Another idea started in Memphis when gas prices had skyrocketed around the country. That's all people were talking about. During the "golden days of radio," station bumper stickers and t-shirts were hugely popular promotional items. When used properly, they created top awareness for radio stations. Stations were always searching for a way to increase bumper stickers on cars. Gas sales got that done well. I remember during a promotion meeting, Bobby OJay mentioned the idea, and that's how it came to life. At the time of our first sale, the cost of gasoline was moving toward $1.50 per gallon.

We decided to sell it for just ten cents. We went to a local gas station chain and told them that we would provide radio advertising to them for the difference between 10 cents and the current gasoline price. So, if the price of gas was $1.45, we would provide them with $1.35 in advertising for every gallon of gas we pumped. The gas sales would last for four hours. Listeners would need a bumper sticker on their car to get the discount. We offered an advertising package to local retailers that would allow listeners to pick up a free bumper sticker.

We picked a gas station that provided us with the ability to manage traffic because we knew people would line up early. The first gas sale was announced on a Friday at 6:00 p.m., and cars began to line up at 4:00 a.m. the next Saturday morning. We had to bring in additional police officers to manage. All the station's DJs and sales staff pumped gas during the sale. It was one of the most successful promotions the station did during my six years at WDIA. We had a gas sale twice every year while I was there, and each one got bigger than the last.

In Houston, at Majic102, we sold gasoline for $1.02 per gallon. The first gas sale at Majic had over three hundred cars lined up by the time it began.

Pay Your Bill

Another health, heart, and pocketbook idea was born as a commitment to help people in need. We asked WDIA listeners to send us a copy of a bill that they wanted us to pay. Every day during the morning show for around three weeks, we read a letter from a listener, and we paid their bill. We literally received thousands of bills each time we did this promotion. It was an example of the power of Black radio to connect with its listeners.

We had a philosophy at WDIA and Majic 102 about what things would be accepted by our listeners. That philosophy was to be sure that our events and promotions always involved things important to our core audience. We felt these programs were what our audience wanted and appreciated.

The Story of Jerry Canty

Jerry Canty was an African American journalist who lived in Houston and worked for Reuters. He'd been traveling back from a Jamaican vacation with his family on a chartered Continental Airlines flight. Sometime after the flight took off, a flight attendant got into a verbal altercation with a passenger sitting in front of Jerry. It was an argument about a boom box the passenger was using. When it got heated, Jerry rose to the defense of the passenger behind him. After more back-and-forth, the flight attendant called the cockpit, and the flight was diverted to Cancun, Mexico. Jerry and the unruly passenger were escorted off the plane and arrested by Mexican authorities—then jailed. The plane left with Jerry's family still on board and returned to Houston.

Jerry was found guilty of flight interference and sentenced to fourteen months in federal prison, plus three years of supervised release. Activist and Houston Councilman Jew Don Boney came to my office one day to tell me about what had happened. For Jerry, the only way out of prison was a pardon by the U.S. Justice Department. I immediately went on the air with an editorial about Jerry's situation. Much like the effort to have listeners sign a petition on behalf of fifteen-year-old Ronald Ward, I asked our listeners in Houston to do the same in support of Jerry Canty. We collected thousands of signatures.

Jew Don was able to arrange a meeting with then-Attorney General Janet Reno. During that meeting, we asked for her support on Jerry's behalf. We had a good meeting with Janet, but we could never get her to move on a pardon approval. Almost two years after he was arrested and put in a Mexican jail, Jew Don and I escorted Jerry Canty and his wife to Carville, Louisiana, where he served out his time in a minimum-security prison.

Haiti-Rwanda Relief Effort

In 1994, Rwanda was locked in a genocide war. At the same time, the island of Haiti was suffering from a brush with Hurricane Gordon that killed over 2,000 people. Both countries were in dire need of food and medical supplies. In collaboration with the local Haiti Recovery Project, the radio station set up relief drop-off stations, where listeners could leave canned goods, non-perishable foods, clothing, and medical supplies. In a month, we were able to collect so many supplies that our local congresswoman, Shelia Jackson Lee, had a U.S. Army cargo plane land in Texas to pick up all we'd collected. It was estimated to be over $300,000 worth of relief items.

The Story of Jamie Green

Jamie Green was a twelve-year-old boy who lived in the historic Third Ward of Houston. His mother was a single mom who was having difficulty raising three children. Jamie spent his 1995 summer cutting lawns to buy himself a new bicycle so he could ride to school. On the first day of school, someone tried to take his bike from him. He refused to give it up, and he was shot in the back by the thief. He was hospitalized for months and paralyzed from the waist down for the rest of his life. I did an editorial to ask listeners to contribute to a fund for the family's medical bills. We raised over $180,000 in a little over two weeks.

MLK (30th Anniversary Assassination) Celebration

When Martin Luther King Jr. went to Memphis in late March 1968 to support the sanitation workers' fight for wages and working conditions, he was assassinated: April 4 at 6:01 p.m., standing on the balcony of the Lorraine Motel.

After spending six years in Memphis, I'd developed a deeper respect for Dr. King and what he did for people of color in America. I will never forget the first time I visited the Lorraine Motel. I had been in Memphis for about a month when I found the time to drive to the motel for a look. It was growing dark by the time I arrived at the grounds. The motel had pretty much been abandoned since King was killed. No one wanted to stay in the place where the greatest civil rights leader in our history had been murdered.

The room Dr. King stayed in that night had been preserved, and there was an eerie red light on inside the room. I remember getting a chill as I looked up from the street below. The photo of Dr. King lying on the balcony floor with Jessie Jackson and Rev. Billy Kyle looking across to where the fatal shot came from flashed in my mind. The city of Memphis planned a celebration on April 4, 1998, to commemorate the 30th anniversary of Dr. King's death. I decided to give our Majic 102 listeners an opportunity to participate in that celebration as well.

I got Continental Airlines to agree to provide a charted plane to fly some listeners with a son or daughter to Memphis to take part in the event. We provided advertising time to Continental in return for the cost of the charter. Listeners mailed letters to the radio station telling us why they wanted to take their child to Memphis for the event. We were accompanied on the trip by Councilman Boney and the newly elected Mayor Lee Brown. We were able to march with thousands of others along the same route Dr. King walked the day before his assassination. All the parents and their kids could also tour the National Civil Rights Museum which sits on the site where the Lorraine Motel once stood.

Roll to the Polls

It is an easy task to pick the two most powerful community service efforts we were involved in during my tenure. The first effort was *Roll to the Polls*. Early in 1996, one of my staff members came into my office to say that Lee Brown was in the lobby waiting to see me. Lee Brown had served as police chief in Atlanta, New York City, and Houston. In 1993, he was appointed by President Bill Clinton as National Director of Drug Policy.[1] Lee was moving back to Houston to establish residency, and he intended to run for mayor. He knew about the great work the stations were doing and asked me for my support of his campaign. I told him he had our full support. A year later, Houston found itself amid the most important election of its history.

There were three important items on the ballot. Lee Brown was running to be elected as the first African American in the city's history. There was a referendum to do away with Houston's affirmative action program. And there was also a proposition to use taxpayer money to build a downtown baseball stadium for the Houston Astros, who'd been playing in the Astrodome since 1965. A close friend and colleague, Darryl King, informed me that he was working with Ken Lay; Ken was the CEO of Enron, which wanted to build the stadium. Ken knew it would be critical to get the African American community's support to use public money. Darryl had negotiated an agreement with Lay that would require thirty percent of stadium contracts to go to minority companies. We, of course, supported that idea, so I told Darryl we would help.

He came back later with a check for $45,000 to support an advertising campaign on our radio stations. We provided an additional $30,000 in promotional support for the proposition. Once again, I was on the air with editorials. One supporting a non-partisan voter registration drive before the election and a message about how it was our responsibility to go to the polls and vote. Another editorial contained the voices of John Kennedy, Martin Luther King Jr., and Malcolm X with the sound of a rifle firing as they spoke. It garnered a lot of positive support from the community and some scorn from our political opponents. Our stations were instrumental in registering thousands of new African American voters in the city. But it was even more important to find a way to get those newly registered folks to go to the polls to cast a ballot. That's how *Roll to the Polls* came about.

I called a meeting of some local community leaders in September 1997 to offer the radio station's help in getting people to the polls. We set up a command center at the historic Shape Community Center. At Shape Center, we set up a telephone phone bank with over two hundred phones. We took calls from people all over the city who needed a ride to a voting location. We had volunteer cab drivers throughout the city picking up and returning people. We had a crew of local attorneys on-site and available to assist voters who were being told they couldn't vote for bogus reasons.

It was an amazing effort that resulted in Lee P. Brown being the first African American mayor in Houston. The proposition to do away with Houston's affirmative action program was defeated, and the referendum to use public money to build a downtown baseball stadium passed. For months after the election each time I was at an event with Lee Brown, he would introduce me as the "man who got him elected." It wasn't me; it was the hard work and dedication of a committed group of radio professionals. Once again, we proved that Black radio had the power to impact political, social, and economic change when used in the right way.

Testing for Tickets

Testing for Tickets was the single most important community effort for me. In 1999, Ada Edward, who was serving as a community advisor at the station, explained an article in the Houston Chronicle about the HIV/AIDS epidemic. It shocked me. I knew the epidemic was bad, but I never realized how bad. It was having a devastating impact on the African American community and on black women particularly. Ada asked me what the radio station could do to help with the problem. I told her rather than try to reinvent the wheel, we should invite the organizations who were on the frontlines of the war against the virus and ask them what help we could provide.

Two weeks later, I convened a meeting with twenty-two community-based organizations that were funded and charged with fighting the virus in Houston. The groups told me that the biggest problems they faced were that people who were taking an HIV test were not returning to get their results. A member of the Houston Health Department indicated that only about forty percent of the people returned for their results. Nationally, around fifty percent were returning. A few days after that meeting, I came upon an idea.

Throughout my radio career, I never really understood the power of a radio station t-shirt. But I can tell you, it was powerful. Unlike anything else I outlined in that phenomenon, the outcome proves that fact. I decided to offer an incentive for those who took an HIV test. During this period, those who took a test had blood drawn and the sample sent to a lab. It took two weeks to get the results back. It was clear that whatever motivated someone to take that first step by taking the HIV test, the fear of finding out you might be positive was too much to bear.

After we started offering a t-shirt and a movie pass, the return rate changed dramatically. In just three months of *Testing for Tickets,* the rate in Houston went from 40 percent to almost 70. We continued to promote testing events and the importance of safe sex in public service announcements twenty-four hours a day on radio. We asked all the DJs to get tested and to talk about the importance of getting tested on air. They made public appearances, and we had local sports figures, celebrities, businesspeople, ministers, and others voicing PSAs to encourage people to get tested.

I guess community service was a part of my DNA. It was responsible for so much of the success I had in my career. Those commitments to community service, a game plan that involved hiring good managers and building a work atmosphere that made people passionate, accounted for so much of my success in radio.

The stations in Houston continued to grow in every arena through the end of 1999. Then, rumors began to circulate that the Houston Combo might be up for sale. The consensus among radio people locally and nationally was *why would Clear Channel sell off their most profitable radio properties?* I knew from my years in the business that more often than not, such rumors were rooted in some truth.

In January of 2000, I received a call from Clear Channel's CEO, Mark Mays. That call would begin the end of my broadcast career, or so I thought.

Endings

End of a Broadcast Career

When it was announced the second week of January that Clear Channel was selling its most profitable radio properties, it was a surprise but not a shock. It was the fourth time in my career that a radio station was sold while I was its manager. Although the sale wasn't shocking, the selling price was. Clear Channel had bought the stations for $75,000,000. In five years, we had grown the value by more than five times. The entire broadcasting world was surprised.

Mark assured me that Radio One had every intention of keeping me on after FCC approval of the sale. "After all," he said, "Why would anyone in their right mind not keep someone who had done the job you have?" My contract with Clear Channel included stock options each year based on performance. I had earned stock options every year with the company. The stock options vested five years after you got them. But there was a clause in my contract that stated the stock options would vest immediately after the sale of the station. I felt like I had the best of both worlds. If Radio One kept me, I still had my job, and I could cash in my stock options.

The orderly transition from old owners to new is normally two or three months. It puts the management in a wait-and-see period. Your management style changes in those situations. Your biggest task is keeping managers and employees in good spirits and productive. The potential owners cannot make any changes in the day-to-day operations by law until the sale is approved. At the same time, the owners who are selling are required to maintain normal operations. However, the old ownership is hardly ever willing to spend money on capital improvements other than in an emergency. It truly is a limbo period for the staff. That can become a problem if the approval of the sale lingers, as was the case with KMJQ/KBXX.

I had an excellent group of employees. We held both the revenue and audience ratings together during the transition. One of the great things about working for Clear Channel was they believed in letting their managers manage. There was little or no interference in day-to-day operations. We didn't know if that would be the case with Radio One. The previous deal had been intended to allow Clear Channel to own seven radio stations in Houston. When a company owns seven radio stations in a single market, it could potentially not only have a monopoly on advertising rates but also have one on news and information.

Clear Channel filed a transfer of license application to sell KMJQ/KBXX with the FCC in December of 1999. They'd been getting license applications in three months or less, a process which could take six to eight months. In January, the Justice Department pulled the transfer application from the FCC to investigate the Houston sale. What would usually take three months took nine months. Since my stock options did not vest until the sale finalization, I had to wait. When the sale was announced, Clear Channel stock was selling at $2.80 a share. By the time the sale was approved, the stock was selling at .32 cents a share. I lost close to $450,000 in the value of my stock during the transition.

Even though new owners are not allowed to make changes at the station, there is some communication between the potential owners and the general manager. In this deal, there was little or no communication between the new owners and me. New owners often make a visit to the new station shortly after the intended sale is announced to calm fears from the staff about the change. The new owners always tell the staff there won't be any change; there always is. Three months after the sale was announced, there had been no visit to the station by Radio One Inc. I mentioned this situation to Mark Mays. Only after that did I receive a call from Alfred Liggins, Radio One's CEO. He advised me that he would be making a visit to the stations in a few weeks.

During his short initial visit, Alfred and I discussed three issues. He asked how our radio stations generated such incredible profit margins. We had great audience ratings but hardly spent any money on promotions, including giving away cash on the air. He told me that we spent less promotional dollars than any station they owned, yet we had the best ratings and profits. I explained that our promotion strategy revolved around our commitment to community service. I told him about many of the great community service projects, how our morning show was the catalyst for almost all we did for the community. It's a fact that in radio, a great morning show builds your audience not only for the morning but the rest of the day. At that time, Majic 102 had the number one morning show in Houston. It was remarkable in that we were a Black radio station, catering primarily to an African American audience. Another issue we discussed was *The Tom Joyner Morning Show*. Tom Joyner was known as the "fly jock." He got that name when he worked as the morning show host for KKDA-FM in Dallas.

72 Health, Heart, and Pocketbook

After his morning show, he flew to Chicago's WGCI-FM to do an afternoon show.

It was the talk of the radio world, and everyone wondered how long he would be able to continue. Tom kept to that schedule for an incredible eight years. In 1994, Tom was hired by ABC Radio Network to do a nationally syndicated show. This became a trend and would change the way radio was presented to local listeners forever. A syndicated show is one that instead of being broadcast locally is broadcast over the internet to a satellite and then it makes it to local radio. After Tom's show was uploaded, he was soon on radio stations in every one of the top ten radio markets . . . except Houston.

ABC Radio Network had been trying to get me to put Tom's syndicated show on Majic102 since 1995. I had refused their offer each year. In my discussion with Alfred Liggins, I explained that canceling our morning show in favor of Tom's would have devastating effects on our ratings and revenue. Once again, I reiterated how our *live-and-local* morning format drove ratings for the entire day. He listened, but he didn't hear. I learned that five months later.

The final issue we discussed was my contract. I took the opportunity to remind him that I would not work for Radio One without one. At the time, I was aware of rumors that Radio One Inc. didn't give GMs contracts. By mid-2000, the *Testing for Tickets* HIV project was getting national attention.

One morning, I received a call from Mike Vogel. Mike was a government affairs director for DuPont Pharmaceuticals. DuPont, with the support of AT&T and the NAACP, had provided a grant to a prominent African American filmmaker, Mustapha Khan, to produce a film about the national HIV epidemic. Mike had heard about *Testing for Tickets*. He wanted to visit me and to see and hear about the project in person. The documentary Khan produced and directed was titled *House on Fire*. Mike brought me a copy of it to watch.

It was the most powerful thing I had ever seen, highlighting the effects on people of color. I called Mike after watching the film and told him I wanted several hundred copies of the film to distribute to the organizations we worked with in Houston. They were the ones on the frontlines. He shipped me two hundred copies, and I dispersed them to use in outreach programs. Late December, Mike Vogel checked in with me again to say what a great job he thought we were doing. He asked me if I might persuade some of my other radio colleagues around the country to duplicate the Houstonian effort. I reminded him we were about to be purchased by what would be the largest Black-owned broadcast company ever. With the sale of our stations and several other pending deals, Radio One would own and operate at least eighteen radio properties nationwide.

I thought it could be a public relations blockbuster for Radio One. He asked me to try to set up a meeting with Alfred Liggins. Shortly after, we flew to the corporate office in Baltimore to pitch the idea. Alfred agreed to the plan, but they didn't have anyone to set up and administer the program; I told him I could. It would require some travel that I wanted to start in Atlanta, Los Angeles, and Cleveland, Ohio. Almost immediately I traveled to Los Angeles and Atlanta to get *Testing for Tickets* started. There were three essential elements needed:

1. A committed radio station that was willing to get their DJs tested, provide t-shirts, and would encourage listeners to get an HIV test. The station would also commit to an intense on-air PSA and be required to designate a staff member to work with me to coordinate the program.
2. A commitment from the state or city health department to do the testing and to do follow-ups.

3. A partnership with a local television station and Black newspaper that would help promote testing events and help provide incentives.

In Houston, we used t-shirts packaged with a movie pass or concert tickets. It took at least two trips to each city to get these three things in place. By early January, all three cities were up and testing. The success once again proved the power of Black radio.

Still, by late January, I had no employment agreement with Radio One. Later that month, I traveled to Baltimore for my first budget meeting with them. Before the meeting began, Liggins questioned me about some travel expenses I had incurred. It was somewhere around $3,000 and mostly for airfare. I reminded Alfred he had approved me to start the effort on behalf of the company. Additionally, I reminded him that when I agreed to coordinate the program, I told him it would be necessary to travel to each city and each station. It was quickly obvious that he was no longer interested in sponsoring the program.

After the meeting, I called Mike Vogel to tell him the bad news. He said, "But Ernie, he approved the project when we met with him." After I returned to Houston, Alfred delivered the straw that broke the camel's back; this time with an early morning phone call. It had been a sunny morning, and I was about halfway through my forty-five-minute ride to the station when Alfred called my cell phone. He said that the company had decided to put the Tom Joyner Morning Show on Majic 102. That would mean my entire morning team, which consisted of two air personalities, a show producer, and a news person, would be let go.

I reminded him of our previous conversation but to no avail. I told him it was his company, and we would make it happen. I immediately called Carl Conner, my program director, and asked him to assemble the morning team after their show was over. When they walked into my office, they looked like someone close to them had died. They found out earlier that morning about the change on the internet. Alfred Liggins had made a public announcement on the Friday before calling me. He wanted to get Tom Joyner back on their flagship station WMJM-FM in Washington D.C., and ABC Radio Network agreed. In return, we had become the sacrificial lambs.

It was then clear that I could not work for Radio One. Throughout my twenty-eight-year career, I had never been fired from a job. I had doubled and tripled results every place I had been. I was respected in the cities where I worked, named one of the top twenty African American broadcasters in America. I had commendations from Houston and congressional leaders, but with Radio One, I had no employment agreement, and apparently, no confidence from Alfred Liggins or the people above.

By January 2001, I had pretty much decided. Before I called Liggins, I made another call to Mike Vogel about my pending resignation and about wanting to take *Project W.A.V.E.* (War Against the Virus Escalating) and *Testing for Tickets* national. I asked if he thought his company would provide a grant to continue the work. Since DuPont had been recently purchased by Bristol-Meyers, it might take a few months to make it happen, but Mike assured me that he thought it probable. After I resigned in March 2001, I withdrew most of my lifesavings during the transition until I heard from Bristol-Meyers. By October, I received a grant for $180,000 for *Project W.A.V.E.* I put together an application to start a nonprofit and created a board of directors. My radio career was over.

Who Killed Black Radio?

You may wonder why this question would warrant any discussion. After all, there are still Black radio stations broadcasting as we speak. I submit that Black radio, as it existed in its heyday, has gone the way of the dinosaur. Black stations used to be institutions in the Black community, where Black folks got their news and information first.

They heard the music they loved on Black radio. They heard disc jockeys who sounded like them and who talked to them about things that mattered in their lives. Most often, those things were about health, heart, and pocketbook. During my years in radio, I tried to adhere to that principle because I thought radio should be the driving force for social and political awareness and change. But never at the expense of offering fun and wholesome entertainment. And so, the events and promotions made Black radio what it was. But that was before the fatal bullet was fired.

Ironically, the person who fired the first bullet was none other than President Clinton. Why would he have done that? Clinton signed the 1996 Telecommunications Act.[1] It was the first time that the internet was included in broadcast legislation. In the late 1960s, there was a growing sentiment among republicans in Congress that those early rules and restrictions were outdated, that broadcasters should be allowed to own as many radio stations as they could afford, regardless of the consequences.

The supporters of the act wanted to provide a *pro-competitive* policy so everyone could use information technologies and services.[2] With the new act and the growing power of the internet, syndicated radio was born. And with syndication came the first death blow to local radio. Companies could have a studio in Dallas broadcasting a morning radio show over the air to listeners anywhere in the country. That is what happened with Radio One and Majic 102. It saved the company the salaries of four people. The company providing the syndication charged a fee and was given advertising spots. Soon broadcast owners realized that not only could they replace morning show staff, they could also replace as many live, local radio shows as they wanted.

Imagine the radio owner in Norfolk who could have his entire

Endings 77

broadcast day filled with DJs for less. It saved radio owners millions upon millions, but it also killed Black radio. It killed the kind of Black radio that raised thousands of dollars to help a crippled teenager's family, got a fifteen-year-old Black youth off death row, sold dirt cheap gasoline to its listeners. The Black radio that turned out the largest number of African American voters in the history of Houston to elect a Black mayor died.

Many groups, including the National Association of Black Broadcasters and the National Black Media Coalition, knew the Telecom Act would be a blow to traditional Black radio. Most of them had fought it. Before the act, Black radio ownership and local programming were alive and well. There were the old guards with influence: Ragan Henry, Eugene Jackson, Sid Small, Bishop L.E. Willis, Egmont Sonderling, Percy Sutton, and the pioneer of African American-owned broadcasting, Willie Davis.

In 1995, before the legislation, there were 146 radio stations owned by African Americans. Today there are less than sixty. African Americans own just 2.1% of the more than 10,212 stations. The golden days of Black radio and Black personalities were gone. Never to return. Here is a tribute to some of those great old-timers.

- Martha Jean the Queen: WDIA Memphis, Tennessee
- Rufus Thomas: WDIA Memphis, Tennessee
- Melvin Lindsey: WHUR Washington. D.C. ("Quiet Storm")
- Frankie Crocker: WWRL New York, New York
- Hal Jackson: WNJR Newark, New Jersey
- Dyanna "Ebony" Williams: WBLS New York, New York
- Nat D. Williams: WDIA Memphis, Tennessee
- A.C. "Moohah" Williams: WDIA Memphis, Tennessee
- Jack L. Coope: WVON Chicago, Illinois

- Petey Green: WOL Washington, D. C.

It is said that trends in radio often go through cycles. Many things from history often come around again. Black radio had been the motivation for change, the tools for clean and wholesome entertainment, the first source for Black folks to find news and information relevant to them. It was the victim of the 1996 government . . . and will not return from the dead.

New Beginnings

Project W.A.V.E Goes to the Big Apple

After my resignation, I withdrew much of my lifesavings waiting to hear from Bristol-Meyers. *Project W.A.V.E. Inc.* was granted nonprofit status in June 2001. In September, I received a grant for $180,000 to continue HIV/AIDS testing. The early months after receiving proper status were spent writing the grant proposals and planning a national rollout for *Testing for Tickets*.

I continued to work with Mike and Mustapha for the launch. Both Mike and Mustapha joined the board of directors. Even though I was no longer an employee of Radio One, Atlanta and Cleveland kept working with me. The initiative was getting a lot of attention in communities of color.

Mustapha and I attended several conferences and meetings that summer to promote the program and provide copies of *House on Fire*. We established a lifelong friendship through the process. In addition to our passion for *Project W.A.V.E.*, we had another common interest: photography. In later years, we would travel together photographing the National Parks. The month before I received the grant, Mike said the New York State Health Department had heard about Project W.A.V.E. and was interested in a meeting with me to discuss bringing the program to New York. That was great news for me as my roots were embedded there.

Mike, Mustapha, and I met late September in New York City with Andrea Small. Andrea was the director of the health department at the time. She and her staff were impressed with the presentation we made. They asked me to put together a plan for New York City.

The most important elements of the plan were to find both a Black and a Hispanic radio station to be a part of the program. *Project W.A.V.E.* and *Testing for Tickets* had always targeted communities of color. My successful career and my reputation in broadcast enabled me to get the attention of the GM of New York City's number one Urban Contemporary station, WBLS-FM. On my first trip back to New York, I met with the WBLS staff. The plan had the same commitment as previous arrangements.

The New York City Health Department had a fleet of HIV/AIDS testing vans to use for street testing events throughout the five Burroughs. Their health department had indicated in our initial meeting the vans had been much underutilized. Only about half were being used for testing. Those vans became ideal for *Testing for Tickets* events. Before we started in New York City, all the testing events were set up at health or community centers and other venues. With the vans, we began to set up at parks, malls, playgrounds, and even street corners.

By the beginning of 2002, *Project W.A.V.E.* was utilizing every testing vehicle in the fleet. We were using WBLS radio station t-shirts, Magic Johnson theater tickets, metro ride cards, and anything else we could get our hands on as return incentives. Soon *Project W.A.V.E.* and the NYC Health Department were testing several hundred people every week for HIV. According to the department, our testing numbers were ten times larger than before. The program went so well that toward the end of September the city asked me to start the program in Albany, Syracuse, Rochester, and Buffalo, New York. This was great news for me because I was familiar with much of Upstate New York.

Growing up only an hour and a half from both Rochester and Syracuse, I had fond memories of my early radio days there. In 1974, while working on my radio & television degree, I had an occasion to spend the coldest day of my life broadcasting a college football game. They had been delayed in finishing their stadium before the football season began. It was three degrees above zero when the game started, and it only got colder. Perhaps, that was a not so fond memory of Upstate New York.

I spent ten days traveling by car from Albany to Syracuse, to Rochester, and finally to Buffalo to meet with local stations, health departments, and potential incentive sponsors. It was surreal being there again, working on such an important effort. By the beginning of November, all five cities in New York State were reporting significant testing numbers from the events. On November 7, 2002, an announcement was made that would change the scope of HIV testing in the U.S. and in the world; it would change *Project W.A.V.E.* protocol forever.

Destiny's Child Steps Up for Project W.A.V.E.

The biggest reason for the success of *Testing for Tickets* was the incentives. The fear that they might have the virus and that it might be a death sentence kept many from getting their results. On November 7, 2002, the OraSure Pharmaceutical Company announced the development of an oral HIV rapid test that gave results in just twenty minutes instead of two weeks. That development changed the protocol for HIV testing worldwide. The fear that people lived with for two weeks was reduced to twenty minutes. That was a game changer. *Project W.A.V.E.* then started to offer incentives on the front end of testing, and there was no need to offer anything for returning.

Getting people to take an HIV test became easier and testing numbers skyrocketed in every market. By the end of 2002, *Project W.A.V.E.* was testing for the virus in twelve cities: Houston, Dallas, New York, Albany, Syracuse, Rochester, Buffalo, Cleveland, Los Angeles, Memphis, Nashville, and Atlanta. There was a great deal of energy and resources in the country focused on stopping the epidemic. *Project W.A.V.E.* was one of the national leaders in that effort. Much of the positive effort was because President Clinton's administration took on the war with a laser-like focus. The administration was totally supportive of programs aimed at slowing the virus, so he appointed Sandy Thurman as AIDS Czar for the U.S. to work hand in hand with the U.S. Surgeon General, David Snatcher.

In 2003, the New York State Health Department provided *Project W.A.V.E* a $25,000 grant to conduct a public service campaign in New York City. Later, Mustapha and I flew to Los Angeles to attend a national conference of Black musicians and actors. Our purpose was to get some of the people attending the event to cut television and radio announcements for the campaign. We were able to get several celebs to help. Included in that list was then Snoop Dogg (now Snoop Lion), Mya, Patti LaBelle, Missy Elliott, Cedric the Entertainer, LL Cool J, and Hill Harper to name a few. We purchased radio and television ads to run on our partner stations and purchased billboard ads for the subway.

From 2001 until 2005, I traveled on three-week intervals to all twelve cities in the *Project W.A.V.E.* network. I flew to New York City on Friday, September 6, 2001, to attend a meeting with the health department in lower Manhattan. I spent Saturday and Sunday at testing events in Brooklyn and Queens. I met with the staff at WBLS on Monday, September 10 and then flew back to Houston that evening. I was in my office the morning of September 11 when a commotion in the lobby caught my attention. I went into the waiting area just in time to witness the attack on the World Trade Center. I had just been in lower Manhattan. I had to leave the office that day, as did almost everyone else in the building, and it was hard to get anything done the rest of that week.

Some of my former staff members at Majic102 and a few local supporters, including Congresswoman Shelia Jackson-Lee, had been working on a fundraising event for *Project W.A.V.E.* since August. The event had been scheduled for the Hilton hotel ballroom in Houston just two weeks after 9/11. It was difficult to get people's time, attention, and money for the event they'd planned.

I remember the night of the fundraising event very well. It was poorly attended, to say the least. As I began my closing remarks, I remember thinking that not only was I not going to raise any money, I was probably going to lose money. Shortly before I finished my remarks, I noticed someone enter the ballroom and take a seat in the back of the room. It was Matthew Knowles: the father of Beyoncé Knowles, and the CEO of Music World Entertainment. Beyoncé and Destiny's Child had been huge supporters of *Project W.A.V.E.* during its early days in Houston. They had personally visited many testing events and had done public service announcements for both our local radio partners as well as those in other cities. Matthew had come to present me with two checks: $10,000 from Music World Entertainment and another $10,000 from Destiny's Child. Those two checks saved the day, and Matthew and Destiny's Child continued to be big supporters throughout the rest of the project's run.

In January 2001, when President Clinton left office, the national support and energy for HIV testing began to die out. This can be attributed to the new administration's feelings in Washington.

84 Health, Heart, and Pocketbook

George H. W. Bush's administration thought the way to solve the crisis was abstinence. So, the national government's support faded rapidly. The AIDS Czar was gone and so too was a lot of funding. Despite that, *Project W.A.V.E.* continued to test and counsel people with *Testing for Tickets* events. Federal support had become so poor that it appeared the project might not survive.

Regardless, on June 27, 2004, (National HIV Testing Day), *Project W.A.V.E.* tested 5,122 people in a single day. We used 259 testing locations with the support of twenty-three media partners. By the time *Project W.A.V.E.* ended in early 2005, we had tested 85,987 people for HIV and had impacted over 132,000 people in our outreach programs. It would take another call from Mike Vogel in February 2006 to commit me to a different but equally important community service endeavor.

Together Rx Access

During my conversation with Mike, we discussed several potential strategies for *Project W.A.V.E.* as George Bush was winding down his first term. Government funds, grant money, corporate donations were all drying up. I received my third grant from Bristol-Meyers for $90,000, half of what the first two grants had been. Support from pharmaceutical companies, which were making billions of dollars selling HIV/AIDS drugs to infected people, was also drying up.

Mike and I talked about potential options. One was to find an organization that could benefit from a fifteen-city network with testing and outreach capability already in place. Before the year ended, Mike had found one. As a government affairs director, Mike was in contact with a lot of people in the healthcare field.

One of the contacts he'd made was with Amy Niles. Amy was a director and board member of Together Rx Access. Together Rx Access was a consortium of pharmaceutical companies that created a free prescription saving card for individuals and families who had no health insurance. It had some of the major pharma players involved, including Pfizer, Abbott, Johnson & Johnson, and Glaxo Smith Kline. They were using marketing companies to drive events and register uninsured individuals. In conversations with Amy, Mike found out that the consortium was having issues getting the card into the hands of people of color. Mike told Amy about the *Project W.A.V.E* network and asked her to call me.

We talked on the phone for two hours before she asked for a meeting in New York to plan how we'd present *Project W.A.V.E* to her board of directors. Together Rx Access would contract with *Project W.A.V.E.* to do the outreach events.

In the first phone conversation, I'd asked Amy why she thought TRXA was having trouble enrolling people of color. What were they doing to attract that group? She said they set up tables at health fairs. Then, what did the enrollment assistants looked like? She said they were usually young White females, many of whom were nursing school students. I immediately told her that was the problem. I suggested that *Project W.A.V.E* would hire people of color as marketing assistants, and they would attend events targeted specifically to minority communities. They would not sit behind a table but instead would walk the floor with clipboards to register people. I reminded her that potential cardholders were more likely to be approachable if the marketing assistants looked like them. She agreed.

Two months later, I packed up all the results from our successful five-year run with *Project W.A.V.E.*, and I headed back to New York for the TRXA quarterly board meeting. My dog-and-pony show was well-received. One month later, I signed a one-year contract with them. When *Project W.A.V.E.* ended, we'd been in fifteen cities around the nation. We had relationships with radio stations, health departments, community-based organizations, and newspapers that were already serving our target communities.

With TRXA, we didn't have to create events where we could enroll people. We could go to radio station events, health fairs, job fairs, concerts, nail salons, and county fairs. I hired a marketing coordinator in each city we were in. Some people I hired were former employees of my radio stations; many had been a part of *Project W.A.V.E.*

Each person had to play a part in the simple but thorough process. Since the TRXA card was free, you had to answer five eligibility questions to get it. The marketing assistants with a clipboard in hand asked questions and then had them fill out the form. It took less than five minutes to complete, where the assistants kept the applications and turned them in to the marketing coordinator.

The market coordinators each had a group of ten to twenty marketing assistants for events. The coordinator checked for accuracy and sent them to the processing center. They had compensation with an event fee, an hourly wage, and $1.00 for every application they turned in. The individual was then mailed their card within two weeks, which offered up to a 40% discount on thousands of prescription drugs.

We started doing events late-2006 in Houston and Memphis. During the last three months, we submitted 4,622 applications and enrolled 8,912 individuals. Applicants could enroll themselves and up to eight additional family members for a total of nine enrollments.

In 2007, I added Atlanta and Dallas; in 2008, New Orleans and Miami; and in 2009, New York, San Antonio, and Orlando. I also went to large annual health fairs in Detroit, Washington D.C., Cleveland, Los Angeles, and St. Louis. In those cities, I traveled there and hired the assistants for a one or two-day event. When I got the contract with TRXA, there were twenty-one other contractors working for them. We finished last at twenty-one enrollments in

2006. By 2009, we moved up to fifth with 26,102 applications and 44,755 enrollments.

I discovered soon after I started the program that the pharmaceutical companies were in this effort for good public relations. I think that angle was more important to them than how many people they were helping. That became more obvious the year after Barack Obama was elected. In 2009, the talk of Obamacare being a reality caused the true colors of Big Pharma to show. The companies did not like Obama, and they did not want Obamacare. We began to hear rumors that they were going to do away with TRXA after Obamacare came into play.

In 2010, we garnered 44,200 applications and 61,128 enrollments to become the number-two contractor. In early 2011, Amy informed me it would be my last year. The pharma companies were pulling the plug. In that last year, we turned in 51,300 applications and enrolled 73,442 people. That was done with a staff of ten market coordinators and approximately 120 marketing assistants. As the year came to an end, I wondered what was next for me.

Beans4Good

When Together Rx Access ended, I felt I still had something to offer an employer. From the time I landed my first job at eighteen as a hospital attendant until December 2010, I'd never been unemployed, never fired from a job, and never in a situation where I was looking for one. With an excellent career in radio and another ten years running two highly successful marketing companies and nonprofits, I still had something to offer an organization. My youngest son, Matthew, who was then twenty-five, reminded me on several occasions how hard it would be for me to find meaningful employment at my age. He had graduated from Stephen F. Austin University with a business degree and an emphasis in human resources. It didn't take me long to realize he was right.

For all of 2011, not only did I not find employment, but I also never got an opportunity to interview. In early 2013, I met someone who was looking to sell a local coffee company. The company, Beans4Good, was helping local nonprofit organizations raise money selling coffee. I thought it was a great idea. It was a new approach to fundraising, different from selling traditions like cookies, candy, and flags. I spent a couple of months with the owner trying to figure out exactly how I could expand what for him had been a part-time job. The coffee he sold was roasted and packaged locally in Houston. He had developed great marketing materials, too. He had logos, packaging materials, signs, brochures, and many other support items. He was willing to sell everything to me. I think he realized he would never be able to grow the business to where he wanted it by doing it part-time.

He sold me the business and all the marketing materials for $2,500 and a share of the revenue for three years. With the help of a colleague, I began to look for a small business loan to grow and expand the business. We were never able to make that happen. I was once again in the position of using lifesavings to keep the business afloat. I didn't know much about the coffee business. What I did know was that every nonprofit organization had one thing in common; they need money and always looked at new ways to raise it.

The coffee was well-received by everyone who bought it. The twelve-ounce bags we sold were no more than a week or two out of the roaster. But there was one problem that I couldn't overcome. Even though nonprofits needed ways to raise money, almost all of them did not have the capacity to sell coffee. They had no sales force and depended mostly on volunteers who couldn't be in a dedicated sales force. The organizations that did have the capacity, like the Girl Scouts and Boy Scouts, were not willing to take on a new product even as good as the coffee was. I could get a few places on board during the first few months, but it became crystal clear after six months, that with no funding and no loan, it would be hard to make Beans4Good a profitable enterprise.

I decided not to put any more of my own money into the business late-2011. In January 2012, something happened at Texas Southern University's public radio station, KTSU-FM, that would eventually thrust me back into radio.

Again in Radio

Trouble at KTSU-FM

KTSU broadcasts at 90.9 on the FM dial and licensed and housed on a university campus. In my broadcasting career, I had always worked at commercial radio stations focused on selling advertisements for profit. Public radio stations owned by public institutions like colleges, universities, and churches get support from the public, including businesses, but cannot sell commercials. Public radio station announcements cannot solicit listeners to buy products or services.

The Corporation for Public Broadcasting (CPB) is a Washington-based nonprofit organization that oversees all public radio stations in the nation. Ninety-five percent of its funding comes from Congress.[1] Both the CPB and NPR (National Public Radio) were formed by Congress in 1970.[2] NPR is under the umbrella of the CPB. NPR provides services like newscasts, educational and musical programs, and documentaries for many public stations and programs in over 1,000 locations, which stations can use like their own.

Since public stations cannot compete with commercial ones, the task of generating revenue is extremely difficult. One way, public stations raise money is through on-air fundraisers. They usually conduct two such events each year in the spring and fall. An on-air campaign is like a telethon but on radio and is usually held for a week. Radio personalities encourage listeners to become a member by making a monetary contribution. The station is permitted to give away products provided by local businesses as incentives to donating members.

In January 2013, KTSU was finishing the audit of its 2012 fall fundraising campaign when trouble popped up. During a radio campaign, when listeners call to donate, they are transferred to a staff member, who takes their pledge. Credit cards and checks are usually accepted. It was discovered that two radio station DJs had stolen donors' credit card numbers to make purchases for themselves and family members. The DJs were suspected to have stolen well over $50,000 from the telethon.

The DJs were fired, and the longtime GM suspended and moved to another part of campus. After a long investigation, one of the DJs, who'd had a previous criminal record, was indicted for credit card theft. The GM's contract was not renewed, and several months later, the university posted the job opening.

I was very familiar with KTSU from my days at Majic102 and KBXX. We had worked with KTSU on various community events. In 1999, Majic102 raised $13,000 to establish a scholarship at Texas Southern University. It was to be named after the station's former news director, Leroy Patterson, a.k.a. Ambikshi Jabarri. So, right there in my hometown was another broken station in need of a fix. It wasn't the same situation I confronted with most commercial radio stations. But, I knew KTSU had tremendous untapped potential. At the time, KTSU was number fifteen in Houston audience listening.

Not unusual for a public station with limited power in a major market. It did have an advantage that no one else had.

KTSU had an exclusive format—jazz. If you could chase all your competition away in a particular musical format, you would be very successful. Houston was the fourth largest city in the nation yet the only one that had no commercial jazz station. When CBS Radio moved away from jazz two years earlier, it had left a void in the market. I felt like KTSU, even as a public station, had an enormous opportunity to fill that void.

I applied for the GM job. I was well-known and still had an outstanding reputation from my work at Majic 102 and KBXX. Many radio people thought I would be a shoo-in and had encouraged me to apply. From the very beginning of the process, something did not seem quite right. The job was posted then taken down.

KTSU had been a part of the Texas Southern School of Communication. After the investigation, the radio station was put under the office of the university president. Eva Pickens, the university's communication director and presidential assistant, became responsible for the station. Because of the scandal, as well as other problems that came to light during the investigation, she headed a fifteen-member search committee charged with finding a new manager in the shadows. By the time interviewing began, a manager hadn't supervised day-to-day operations for almost a year. Who was being interviewed and when they were interviewed was a well-kept secret.

On April 13, 2013, I was called to the campus for the interview. In my twenty-seven years interviewing for management jobs, I had never had one by a search committee. In commercial stations, owners make the decision about the hiring and firing. I was well-prepared, and during the two hours, I laid out my plan for KTSU. Something happened at the end that had never happened during my entire career in radio. The search committee stood and clapped.

I asked but wasn't told when a decision would be made about the job. After the interview, the committee immediately sent me to meet the Dean of the School of Communication. The first question he asked me was if I got the job, was I willing to fire everyone at the station and start over with a new staff. I told him I would do the same thing I had done my entire career. I would begin by interviewing every single employee, full-time and part-time. From there, I would decide who the players would be as we moved forward. He told me he could have picked a manager himself, but he'd wanted to let the university community be a part of the decision. He then said, "Ernie to be honest with you, I don't know what I will do if they don't choose you." I thanked him for the opportunity and asked him when a decision would be made. He said it would be made before the end of the month.

That was the last time I heard from him or anyone else at the university. No call, no letter, no email, no thank-you-for-coming. Six months later, Eva Pickens hired a manager. I cannot tell you the number of people who asked me during the months after, "Why didn't you get the job?" Later, with some additional information given from people close to the process, I realized why. It was clear to those responsible for deciding that the radio station was broken. They knew there was still unethical and perhaps illegal activity going on at the station. I know that it was apparent to the decision-makers, all that would come to an abrupt end if I was hired, and there were people who were personally benefiting from that unethical activity.

They passed on me, so I moved on.

Back in the Saddle Again

In early April of 2014, while I was waiting to hear from the KTSU, I was doing some research into the problems at Texas Southern. I remembered having met a young lady who had worked there in 2000 and left KTSU to take a job as GM at KPVU-FM. KPVU is the public radio station licensed to Prairie View A&M University, a historically Black university founded in 1876 and the first state-supported institution for African Americans in Texas.

KPVU went on the air in February 1982 at 91.3 on the dial. As a low power station (31,000 watts), there were large parts of Houston where the station could not be heard. When I called to speak to Cheryl Brooks to get some information about her experience, I was told she was no longer employed at the station. I wondered if her job had been filled and was told it had not. KPVU was physically housed in the school of communication at Prairie View, but it was not a part of the school. The radio station was a part of auxiliary services at the university and abandoned by the school of communication some years ago due to issues related to fighting and other misbehavior.

I contacted Anitra Addison who was the assistant director of auxiliary services to inquire if and when there would be a search for a new manager. Anitra knew about me from my radio work in Houston. She said that the job would be posted in a couple of weeks and encouraged me to apply. It was posted three weeks later, and I did apply. There was no search committee to deal with, so Anitra would decide. In late May, I had my interview, and on June 4, I started my first day as the GM of KPVU. I was back in the saddle after a thirteen-year absence from radio. And once again, I was charged with doing what I did best, fixing a broken radio station.

KPVU was completely broken. It was forty miles from a major metropolitan area, the signal was weak, and the station had no music direction, playing blues, gospel, jazz, and R&B. They also were at risk for losing their funding. All public radio stations are required to meet certain audience ratings and fundraising goals each year to qualify for CPB funding, and the station had not met its CPB goals for two consecutive years. If a station does not meet its goals for three years, it may lose backing. Not only had the station not met those goals, it had sent back unused funds. CPB support for KPVU amounted to well over fifty percent of the total dollars to the station. There was no general manager, no plan to increase revenue, and few if any people were listening to the station. They were flying by the seat of their pants.

My first priority was to put together a plan to grow revenue through the annual fundraising campaigns. The second was to change the programming from what could best be described as a hodgepodge to something people really wanted to listen to. It did not take me long to realize the source of the revenue problem. The station's fundraising director did not have a clue about how to grow the station's revenue. Had the radio station been a commercial station, I would have fired her immediately. Because the station was a part of the university and not operated independently, it was difficult to terminate employees without having to jump through hoops. I had to build a case in writing how I was justified in firing her. That took three months. She appealed my firing, and it took another three months for her to exhaust her appeal.

It was clear that working in public radio, especially at a university, would be daunting. During my commercial radio career, I alone could change all aspects of the day-to-day operations. Not so in public radio. Almost every decision needed to improve operations quality had to be cleared through a long and slow approval process. It was very frustrating. I was trying to move at the speed of a Learjet, but the university was moving at the speed of a Conestoga wagon.

I decided to change the musical format from a hodgepodge to smooth jazz. The response was well-received by most of the campus community. A rumor had been circulating for some time about why there was not a good signal. It speculated the antenna on the radio's tower was pointed in the wrong direction away from Houston. That was not true. The reason the station did not have a good signal was due to the low height of the radio tower in combination with the station's low power.

Again in Radio 97

I knew the way to get a stronger signal was to raise the height of the radio tower or move it closer to Houston. A combination of both would be even better. It was unlikely, however, since it was in the flight path to the airport. It would be almost impossible to get the approval of the FAA (Federal Aviation Administration). I hired a radio engineering firm to do a study to see if it were possible to move the tower closer or find a closer tower that had room on it to relocate our radio antenna. Locating one would be much less expensive than finding a piece of land to build on. The engineering firm did find a tower that looked like it might work, but I put that project on hold and continued to work on getting the new format to where it should be.

It was a daily grind, fixing that radio station. Nothing was easy. There was one thing that did bring some good moments during my short time at KPVU. In addition to the music, news, and NPR programming we carried, we also carried Prairie View A&M football. The Prairie View Panther football team plays in the Southwestern Athletic Conference (SWAC). Each year, the university and the station manager had a bidding process to decide who the broadcast team would be for the football season.

Leonard Moon, who owned a local sports marketing company, had won the bid to do Panther games the four previous years. After listening to the games, I decided I would use Leonard for the 2014 season as well. Leonard had done a great job, but the games were awful from a technical standpoint. As soon as I took the time to look at the broadcast equipment, I knew why. It was antiquated and broken. I made two decisions immediately that I knew would improve broadcast quality. I purchased some new state-of-the-art digital equipment and upgraded the commentator.

The color commentator for the games was different every year, and Leonard did the away games by himself. I hired a teacher who had played football at Prairie View. I then added a third member of the broadcast team to be a sideline reporter. That person was me. It had been thirty-six years since I had done my last sports broadcasting while I was at WTKO in Ithaca. On Friday night during football season, I enjoyed winding down from the long weeks at work, doing what I loved . . . calling football games.

The university had put a cap on spending for the PVU broadcast of football games. It was not high on their priority list. To work a three-man team into the budget, we all traveled in a university van to all the away games. That fall of 2014, I drove to Jackson and Itta Bena, Mississippi; Pine Bluff, Arkansas; Birmingham, Alabama; and Baton Rouge, Louisiana. I loved it. I was back in the saddle again.

The response was overwhelmingly positive. Also, for the first time in three years, KPVU did not have to return money to the CPB. But it was clear the station was likely to lose its funding in 2015 for not meeting its audience rating and fundraising goals. I wrote a lengthy letter to the CPB vice president of operations, detailing all the problems at Prairie View that had led to the KPVU's failures. As a result, the university and the station were given an extra year to get things in order.

In a meeting with Anitra Addison, in the spring of 2015, I offered a detailed plan on what it would take to continue to get the KPVU back in compliance. Three months later, no approval for the plan had been given. It was clear the university didn't really care about the success or failure of its radio station. On August 4, 2015, I resigned as the radio manager of KPVU after only sixteen months at the job.

Have Camera Will Travel

Life as a Photographer

Throughout all the joys and challenges in my career, my love for photography never left. Growing up a country boy, living in the beautiful Finger Lakes, I knew the lakes well. There are thirteen narrow ones, running north to south. Seneca Lake is the biggest; Canadice Lake is the smallest, which had been home of the Iroquois Indians. The area is now the largest wine-producing region in New York with over a hundred wineries. My house was just a mile from the lakeshore. I woke every day looking at this incredible landscape, where I could fish and enjoy time with Rosie.

I have fond memories of taking pictures as a youngster when our family traveled to the many state parks that surrounded us. Most of those photos were of our family rather than the parks. I bought my first real camera in the early part of 1970, a Minolta, precursing a serious interest in photography as an art form. The Kodak Kodachrome came next and got me that best-in-class at Ithaca. Glen

State Park, which won me the A+, was a place my mother took us as youngsters for picnics and hikes. It contains a nearly three-mile-long gorge that has over 2,000 steps that take you through waterfalls and steep canyons. I would photograph the Watkins Glen gorge many times during my travels back to Upstate New York.

**Ernie Jackson in Death Valley National Park, January, 2018
Photo taken by Mustapha Kahn**

In 1989, when I moved to Norfolk, two things advanced both my photography interest and skills. Throughout most of my adult life, I'd wanted to own an RV. When I was living in Memphis, there was an RV dealer only a few blocks from where we lived. I would often visit the dealership to just look over some of the motor homes they had. I had almost decided that I would start my RV life by buying a *pop-up*.

A pop-up is a small camper that can be easily towed with a car and unfolds when you set it up at a campground. It is a small and tight place to live in.

That was pretty much what I had decided to do until a winter storm in February of 1992 hit Memphis with eight inches of snow. On my way back from work after that storm, I passed the RV dealership and noticed a sign saying they were having a winter storm sale. I found a twenty-seven-foot Class A motor home that was selling for $15,000 off the sticker price, so I bought the RV. It was a beauty manufactured by Rexhall, a model called the Aerbus. I will never forget the first trip we made in the Aerbus; I named it MR HEW. Those letters stood for my son Matthew, my mother Rosie, Hulda, Willda's mother, and William, Willda's father.

On our first family trip, we were headed from Memphis to Kentucky Lakes on the Tennessee-Kentucky border. It was a five-hour trip. About three hours in, the RV stalled out on the interstate, and we lost all power. We had to have the RV towed to the nearest town, where we rented a car to return to Memphis. The RV was later towed back to the dealership. I continued to have intermittent power failure with MR HEW, but despite that, we traveled as often as we could to state parks in Tennessee and Mississippi.

My mother loved riding in MR HEW. She was always ready to go whenever I suggested a trip somewhere. During my six years in Memphis, we made a number of trips from Tennessee down the Blue Ridge Parkway in Tennessee and North Carolina. The Blue Ridge Parkway is a photographer's heaven. We would find small quaint campgrounds to stay at there. It was during this time that I really began to fine-tune my photography skills. When we moved to Norfolk, we were even closer to the parkway and spent even more time camping there.

The second thing nice about Norfolk was having my professor at

Norfolk State introduce me to a new film he was using, the Fuji Velvia. I had been using the Kodak Kodachrome, which produces a film negative from which you make prints. Velvia was a slide film, which produced a slide image of a much better quality than a negative. The color saturation created was incredible. After my professor gave me a roll to try, I used it, and I never shot another roll of Kodak Kodachrome in my life. Over the next four years, I started my portfolio of images from several national parks, including Smokey Mountain National Park, Grand Canyon National Park, Shenandoah National Park, and Haleakala National Park.

When I moved to Houston, the radio stations offered *Big Trips* to our radio advertisers for spending extra ad dollars during the first quarter each year. The first quarter is always the toughest time to grow revenue at a radio station. The idea of *Big Trips* was the owner John Lynch's idea. He loved to travel and so did I, so it was great for me and increased my portfolio. The first three years, *Big Trips* took us to Spain, Italy, and an excursion on the famous Orient Express. The following year, we took family trips to Hawaii, Portugal, and Greece. By 1995, I had a fairly good-sized photography portfolio.

I never really thought that my photography was good enough for people to want to purchase. That changed in 1996, when I met Sharon Barnes, an African American woman in charge of buying artwork for one of Houston's leading hospitals: St. Luke's. She had come to my office one day for a meeting. I had some of my photographs on the walls, including several from Greece. She asked me where I had purchased the pictures, and when I told her they were mine, she asked if I had others.

A few weeks later, I went to her office with my portfolio, and she bought thirteen photographs for the hospital, including five from Greece. The hospital was converting a conference room to honor a retiring Greek doctor. Twenty years later, after my wife had surgery to remove a tumor from her left lung, I was visiting her late one evening. She had been moved to a different wing of the hospital, and when I stepped off the elevator to the waiting area, there were eight of the photographs Sharon Barnes had purchased. I had no idea that they were still there.

I have had two opportunities to have my photography displayed in different galleries here in Texas. I was invited to be a featured artist for two years at the DaVinci Artists Gallery, a gallery of about fifteen local artists in Tomball. The gallery was off the beaten track and had little traffic. Some Saturdays when I worked, there may not have been more than four or five people coming into the gallery. I enjoyed my time there but had very few sales. I was also asked to exhibit my photography at the Johnson Library on the Prairie View A&M University campus for six months in 1994.

National Parks

The United States has sixty-three protected areas known as national parks.[1] For almost all my life, there were only fifty-nine. In 2018, Donald Trump designated two additional state parks, one in Indiana and one in Illinois. What made him decide to do that still remains a mystery to most people. I am sure it had something to do with money, and the money went to him.

Our national parks are operated by the National Park Service, an agency of the Department of the Interior, and they are established by Congress.[2] "A bill creating the first national park, Yellowstone, was signed into law by President Ulysses S. Grant in 1872."[3] Sequoia and Yosemite became national parks in 1872 and 1890 respectively.[4] The National Park Service was formed from the Organic Act of 1916.[5] There are seven national parks, which include six in Alaska and are paired with a national preserve. National parks and preserves are administered together but are considered separate units and have different levels of protection. Other units of the National Park Service (421 altogether), do not hold formal titles but are broadly referred to as national parks.[6] They include monuments, battlefields, historic sites, scenic trails, recreational areas, and seashores.

Along with the U.S. Virgin Islands and the American Samoa territory, twenty-nine states have national parks: California has nine, Alaska has eight, Utah has five, and Colorado has four.[7] Wrangell-St. Elias in Alaska, the biggest national park, is over 8 million acres.[8] Gateway Arch National Park in Missouri is the smallest park at only 192 acres.[9] The total protected area is approximately 52.2 million acres.[10]

In 2017, the national parks had more than 84 million visitors, setting a record.[11] Another record was in 2018 with a 2% increase. The most visited national park is the Great Smoky Mountains National Park in North Carolina and Tennessee. Over 12.5 million people visited this park in 2017. Arizona's Grand Canyon National Park is the second most visited park. Over 6 million people visited that park in 2017.

It is interesting to note that the first two national parks I photographed were Grand Canyon National Park and Smoky Mountain National Park. Here is the list of locations operated that I have visited and or photographed:

- Statue of Liberty: New York, New York
- Boston African American Historic Site: Boston, Massachusetts Acadia National Park: Maine
- Gettysburg National Military Site: Gettysburg, Pennsylvania
- Women's Right's National Historical Park: Seneca Falls, New York

- Boston National Historical Park: Boston, Massachusetts
- Vanderbilt Mansion National Historic Site: Hyde Park, New York
- Delaware Water Gap National Area: Bushkill, Pennsylvania
- Assateague Island National Seashore: Ocean City, Maryland
- Shenandoah National Park: Northern Virginia
- Washington Monument National Memorial: Washington, D.C.
- Gauley River National Recreation Area: West Virginia
- New River Gorge National River: Fayetteville, West Virginia
- Natchez Trace Parkway: Mississippi
- Blue Ridge Parkway: Asheville, North Carolina
- Fort Sumter National Monument: Charleston, South Carolina
- Great Smoky Mountain National Park: Gatlinburg, Tennessee
- Grand Portage National Monument: Grand Portage, Minnesota
- Buffalo National River: Marshall, Arkansas
- Hot Springs National Park: Hot Springs, Arkansas
- San Antonio Missions National Park: San Antonio, Texas
- Grand Canyon National Park: Grand Canyon, Arizona
- Rocky Mountain National Park: Ouray, Colorado
- Petroglyph National Monument: Albuquerque, New Mexico
- Zion National Park: American Fork, Utah
- Death Valley National Park: Death Valley, California

- Muir Woods National Monument: Mill Valley, California
- Yosemite National Park: Modesto, California
- Haleakala National Park: Pukalani, Hawaii
- Crater Lake National Park: Crater Lake, Oregon
- Olympic National Park: Port Angeles, Washington
- Grand Tetons National Park: Jackson, Wyoming
- Yellowstone National Park: Jackson, Wyoming

The national parks are our most precious and most endangered national treasures. I often get asked which are my favorite. Here are the top ten national parks that I have photographed.

Ten: Olympic National Park (Established 1938)—Washington

This is not a drive-through park. No road crosses its heart, though a dozen roads lead into the park. Ninety-five percent of the park is designated as wilderness.[12] The park features high mountains with subalpine forests, alpine meadows, and temperate rain forests. It also has seventy miles of sandy or rocky shoreline.[13] You need four full days to capture all the diversity of this park. It is probably the most diverse park I have shot.

Best time to shoot the park: summer.

108   Health, Heart, and Pocketbook

Nine: Acadia National Park (Established 1919)—Maine

Located on the northeastern side of Maine, this park offers a rugged shoreline with crashing waves, with lighthouses rising above coniferous forests. The park offers incredible photo opportunities with ponds, rivers, carriage roads and bridges, as well as wildflowers, mosses, and ferns.[14] It is also known for its sunrises and sunsets. There is a twenty-seven-mile Park Loop Road where there are photos at every turn.[15]

You need at least four days to shoot here as well. Best time to shoot the park: spring and fall.

Eight: Zion National Park (Established 1919)—Utah

Located in the northwest of Utah, it is one of five national parks in the state. This park would rank higher on my list if I had traveled to shoot it at a different time. I went in the spring, but I went too early. We took a family trip to Zion in 2005. My son Matthew had taken an interest in photography and had his own camera. The trip was an early high school graduation present for him.

Zion is an incredibly humbling place. Much like Grand Canyon National Park. The red rocks and mountains are majestic, and they surround you everywhere. I love shooting leaves in the spring; new spring leaves have a vibrant lime-green color when they arrive. There are not a lot of trees in Zion. There are no forests. But I thought that the trees there, with new green leaves, would make an awesome background for all the giant red rocks in the park. When we arrived, no leaves at all were on the trees yet. We were two weeks early for perfect leaves. Still, it was a great park to shoot.

You can shoot the entire park in two or three days. Best time to shoot the park: summer and fall.

Have Camera Will Travel   111

**Seven: Rocky Mountain National Park (Established 1915)—
Colorado**

Rocky Mountain National Park saddles the Continental Divide and has some of the most spectacular high-mountain landscapes in the United States.[16] Paved roads give access to almost all of the park. The park has more than sixty peaks above 12,000 feet in elevation, 450 miles of streams and rivers, and 150 lakes. The parks also features numerous ghost towns. Most of them had once been mining towns. This was another photography trip that included my son Matthew.

Once we got to the park, we decided to take a backroad Jeep tour into the high mountains. The Jeep was an open-air vehicle that seated twelve. The roads were steep and narrow, and as we climbed to nearly 12,000 feet, you could look straight down over the Jeep's side and see the entire drop. It made Matthew so nervous he hid his head under my jacket. The people on the tour with us later bought Matthew a t-shirt that said, "Houston We Have a Problem." It had his name on it.

The park also has a great train ride from Ouray to Durango. You can sit outside or inside the train. Matthew opted to sit inside. You could spend some time in Durango, which is a wonderful old mining town now filled with tourist attractions.

You need four days to cover most of the park. Fall colors here are spectacular. Best time to shoot the park: summer and fall.

Have Camera Will Travel   113

**Six: Great Smoky Mountain National Park (Established 1934)
—Tennessee/North Carolina**

This park, which is in both Tennessee and North Carolina, covers 814 square miles.[17] No other park of equal size on earth outside of the tropics offers the biodiversity of the Great Smoky Mountain National Park. I have been there taking photos on three different occasions. The park features rugged mountains, mountain streams, rivers, forests, cattle farms, grist mills, spring flowers, and fall colors. You can spend a whole day photographing the small mountain town of Cades Cove at the eastern end of the park. The park is the most visited of the national parks.[18] On the edge, near the center sits the city of Gatlinburg, Tennessee. It is a fun frontier/mountain town with lots of attractions.

You could spend a day just shooting there. You really need five days. Best time to shoot the park: spring (incredible places to shoot spring leaves) and fall. Fall colors here are spectacular.

114 Health, Heart, and Pocketbook

Five: Yellowstone National Park (Established 1872)—Wyoming

This is the *granddaddy* of them all. This is the oldest national park in America.[19] It has every imaginable landscape you could ever want except mountains: waterfalls, wildflower meadows, rivers, lakes, forests, wildlife, including elk and buffalo, which you sometimes have to stop in the middle of the road to let pass. Yellowstone is also a hydrothermal wonderland with steaming thermal pools, bubbling mud pots, and over 300 active geysers. The most famous of these is Old Faithful.[20] You can photograph this park while traveling along a 142-mile, figure-eight-shaped loop.[21]

You need at least three days to shoot. Best times to shoot the park: winter, spring, summer, fall.

Four: Yosemite National Park (Established in 1890)—California

This park is one of the world's most famous places. It is a historic icon of the conservation movement—not just for the United States, but for all nations. The magnificent beauty of its waterfalls, massive rock formations, rushing rivers, giant sequoia trees, and alpine meadows led to calls for its protection in the middle of the late 19th century.[22]

When President Abraham Lincoln in 1864 signed a congressional bill granting Yosemite Valley and the Mariposa Grove of Giant Sequoias to California as an inalienable public trust, it marked the first time that any nation had set aside land as a wilderness preserve.[23] Pioneering landscape photographer Ansel Adams spent a lot of time photographing this iconic park.[24] Maybe the best shot in the park is just outside at Tunnel View Overlook. The picture shows four of the most photographed places in the park. The mountain face of El Capitan, Bridalveil Falls, Half Dome, and the Yosemite Valley. Another of Adam's most famous images is a Yosemite classic view. I stood approximately where he must have stood and took that same shot, which adds the Merced River to all the features that are in the tunnel view photo.

It's possible the single most spectacular photo opportunity is at Yosemite Falls. It is a 2,425-foot waterfall made up of three separate drops: Upper Yosemite Fall, the middle cascades, and Lower Yosemite Fall.[25] These falls are the tallest in North America and the fifth tallest in the world.[26] It is a challenge finding a way to get the entire falls in a single frame. The park has thirteen campgrounds and several lodges, but you cannot get a reservation either between April or September. In 2015, the park stopped letting in visitors, and instead, you now park outside to be shuttled into the park. There are also three separate sequoias groves that are all worth visiting.

You need at least five days to really see this magnificent national park. Best time to shoot: winter, spring, summer, and fall.

Have Camera Will Travel 117

**Three: Grand Teton National Park (Established 1929)—
Wyoming**

There is literally a photo opportunity around every corner in this national park. There are higher mountains in North America, but none more dramatic than the Teton Range. According to National Geographic, because of the manner of their geologic birth, these rugged mountains "rise with near verticality more than 7,000 feet above the valley floor," without foothills impeding views of their rocky slopes and deep canyons.[27] This makes sunrise and sunset photos remarkable, to say the least. Spectacular and easily accessible roads and scenery combined with blue lakes and wildlife, which includes grizzly and black bears, elk, moose, bighorn sheep, and bison, make this one of the most popular parks.[28]

Another great thing about this national park is that it is only thirty minutes from Yellowstone National Park. This park is easy to hike and easy to drive around.

You need three full days to shoot this park. However, you can combine a five-day photo shoot and include Yellowstone. Best time to shoot the park: summer and fall.

**Two: Death Valley National Park (Established 1994)—
California**

It was really hard to decide between the number one and number two best national parks for me. Death Valley was not even on my radar or bucket list until 2017. In that August, I happened to watch a video about this park. I was shocked at the beauty and the diversity. My ideas about the park were the same as most people's. When I was watching the video, it was 115 degrees in Death Valley. I knew I wanted to photograph this park, but I knew it would have to be in winter.

Death Valley is among the world's most geographic names. For most people, it probably seems foreboding, even dangerous, lacking any appeal as a place to visit. I was among those folks until the first day I set foot in the park. Death Valley can be dangerous, but the same can be said of crossing a busy city street. I can tell you from being there myself if you take proper precautions, you have nothing to fear in Death Valley National Park.

"Hottest, driest, lowest" is a common description of Death Valley. There have been years that have no rainfall.[29] The annual average is less than two inches. In July 1913, a temperature of 134 degrees was registered at the site now called Furnace Creek Ranch. It was the hottest temperature ever recorded on earth at the time.[30] In July, the average temperature is 115 degrees.[31] Death Valley has a place called Badwater Basin, where the elevation goes 282 feet below sea level.[32] That makes it the lowest place in America. When I arrived at Badwater Basin, on my second day, I stood below a cliff on desert ground, looking 200 feet above me at a sign that said, "Sea Level."

If you are curious how Death Valley got its name, here is the story.[33] In 1849, a group of pioneers wandered into the valley on their way to California. They endured a two-month-long ordeal of hunger, thirst, and awful silence[34], as they tried to find their way out of the 140-mile-long basin.[35] One man died, the other two assumed their fate would be the same. The National Park Service says they were found and rescued, and "as the party climbed out of the valley, one of the men turned, looked back, and said, 'Goodbye, Death Valley.'"[36] The name stuck.

There is little wildlife in Death Valley except for a few bighorn sheep, coyotes, and roadrunners.[37] In the late 19th century, Death Valley saw wagons haul powdery white borax from mines, which have long since been abandoned.[38] Over the years, miners sought gold, silver, lead, zinc, mercury, copper, salt, manganese, and other minerals there.[39] There are estimated to be nearly 10,000 abandoned mines in the valley.[40] So why would anyone go there hoping to find something to photograph?

The video I watched made me believe there was something special in this place. And there was. I took this trip with my longtime friend Mustapha Khan. We stayed in a small desert resort about twenty-one miles outside the park entrance. We both flew into Las Vegas, rented a car, and made the two-and-a-half-hour drive to the

Longstreet Resort and Casino. The casino was not much bigger than our room. It was January 14, 2018, four days before my seventy-fifth birthday.

We arrived at the resort with about two hours left before sunset and decided to make the drive to the park to have a quick look. As we entered the park from the southeast, we were in awe of what we saw before us. The most incredible light was illuminating the landscape. We couldn't get our cameras out fast enough. We shot until the very last sliver of light was left and headed back to Longstreet in pitch-black darkness, but excited about the possibilities that might lie ahead the next four days. The glimpse we got during our brief stay the evening before was nothing compared to what we witnessed our first full day.

It should be noted that we were in Death Valley during the 2018 government shutdown. Mustapha and I had decided to make the trip despite this fact. I had five days planned out, day by day and spot by spot for this trip. Because of the shutdown, many places we had planned to photograph were not available due to many roads being closed. There were no park rangers on duty, and many of the public toilets were locked up. That, however, did not stop us from what was an incredible five-day photo shoot.

It is hard to describe the grandeur, the colors, the stillness, and the absolute majesty of Death Valley. There were mountains, valleys, rock formations, and vegetation, unlike anything we had ever seen. There were sand dunes, ghost towns, volcanic craters, and incredible sunrises and sunsets. We shot from sunrise to sunset every day. Some of our favorite spots were Zabriskie Point, Mesquite Dunes, Devil's Golf Course, Bad Water Basin, Furnace Creek, Artists Pallet, and Dante's Peak.

It was unforgettable, and Death Valley National Park is one of only two that I intend to return to after having visited it. The other is the number one national park on my list.

One: Crater Lake National Park (Established 1902)—Oregon

Born of a volcano, Crater Lake is one of legendary beauty. All the national parks I have visited have a majestic quality about them. Crater Lake is not only majestic, it is magical. It is the only park I have visited that I would attribute that quality to and is truly one of the scenic wonders of North America. The magic of the park lies in the story told by the Native American tribes (the Klamath) that still inhabit the region.

But first, how did this lake come to be? Crater Lake is the fifth oldest national park in the United States and the only one in Oregon.[41] The lake is 1,949 feet at its deepest point. That makes it the deepest lake in the U.S., the second deepest in North America, and the ninth deepest in the world. Crater Lake doesn't have streams that flow into or out of it.[42] The water comes from rain and snowfall, and evaporation or subsurface seepage is how the water leaves. The lake has the bluest hue of any I have seen. And I have seen quite a few. When it was being formed, about 7,770 years ago Mount

Mazama (part of the Cascade Range) exploded, sending ash miles into the air.[43] So much pumice (molten rocks) and ash was ejected, the Mount Mazama's summit collapsed, creating a caldera up to six miles in diameter and 4,000 feet deep.[44]

The explosion was a hundred times as large as the 1980 blast at Mount St. Helens, also a part of the Cascade Range.[45] It is said many Klamath Indians, several living miles and miles away, died from the eruption.[46] Over the next 740 years, the caldera filled with water to form what is now Crater Lake.[47] There isn't much snow at the lower elevations in western Oregon; however, at the higher elevations, like where Crater lake is, it's common. Measurable snow falls on average 101 days every year. As much as thirty-seven inches of snow has fallen on a single day.

I traveled to Crater Lake in August of 2017. They had only stopped plowing snow from the road around the lake two weeks before I arrived. That winter, it received 484 feet of snow during a three-month period. The average annual snowfall is 463 feet.[48] Crater Lake is about a two-hour drive from Eugene, Oregon. It is a beautiful drive that crosses rivers and streams through pine forests and wine vineyards.

I stayed in a motel in the tiny town of Chemult. Besides the motel, there was only a gas station with a Subway deli and a forest ranger station. During my first morning, I saw plenty of evidence of lingering snow in places even though it was 78 degrees in August. The night before, I had met some forest firefighters at the Subway. They'd just been relieved from a fire they had been trying to control southeast of the park. When I arrived at the park, the lake was obscured by smoke and haze. A ranger at the park headquarters told me an approaching easterly wind would soon blow the smoke away. I decided to have some breakfast and wait it out.

At about 11 a.m., I wandered out of the lodge to take what I hoped would be my first look at Crater Lake. The smoke had cleared and what I saw made me stop and stare. I could not believe that what I saw was real. There before me was the calmest, bluest, most peaceful lake I had ever seen. A magical feeling came over me. That feeling stayed with me for the next four days. I had seen and photographed the Grand Canyon, Grand Tetons, Yellowstone, Yosemite, and the awesome wilderness of Death Valley. All those places were majestic in their own way, but none had the feeling of this park.

It was two days later when I took part in a park ranger lecture that I heard the story about what makes this park magical.[49] The Klamath Indians still tell a story passed down to them about how the park got its incredible blue color. They believed in the mountains and forests there lived two gods. Llao who was the god of the Below World and Skell the god of the Above World. Skell had a beautiful daughter, who Llao spotted one day and immediately fell in love. When he saw her again, he asked her to be with him and care for him. She rebuked his offer, and he became incensed and started throwing fireballs everywhere.

The two Gods then began a prolonged war against each other. During a particularly huge fight, somehow Skell's daughter got caught in the crossfire and was killed. Skell was done with the war. The Indians begged him not to give up because they feared Llao would then kill all of them. Skell agreed to one last battle, and at some point, Skell picked up Llao and hurled him deep into the Below World, which caused the mountain to explode and erupt, spewing molten lava, rocks, and ash everywhere. This was the eruption of Mount Mazama. Llao was finally vanquished; the Indians found peace and prospered.

Thousands of years later, Skell to honor his daughter came down from the sky and dove into the body of water that had filled the caldera: Crater Lake. He changed the water's color to reflect the sky where he'd lived. This is the magic of Crater Lake National Park.

There is a 33-mile-loop road that goes around the lake. There is a view at every turn, and one can see the lake from different angles. Since it lies in a north-to-south line, there are places around the entire lake for incredible sunrise and sunset shots. One of my favorite shots taken is called "Phantom View." A tiny island in the southwestern part of the lake resembles a ghost ship. It is appropriately named Phantom Ship. Another great shot is at a spot just behind the park lodge that looks out to Wizard Island, named so because the island looks like the hat of a wizard.

Other great places to photograph are lookouts at Sentinel Overlook, Garfield Overlook, Castle Creek Pullout, and Cleetwood Overlook. If you only have one choice to visit a national park, make the choice Crater Lake National Park.

You need at least three days to shoot this park. A fourth day would give the opportunity to shoot some waterfalls and hike some rivers. Best time to shoot: summer—August.

I want to add two honorable mentions that didn't quite make the top ten.

The Oregon Coast, Hwy 101 from Seaside to Florence, Oregon

There are two drives you can take for great photo opportunities. One is the Columbia River Gorge Highway (the old highway). It travels east from just outside Portland for about sixty miles to Hood River, Oregon.[50] In Hood River, you can also photograph Mt. Hood. There are more than eighty waterfalls along the old highway. Some you can see and photograph from the highway; others require hikes anywhere from a mile or two to all-day journeys. Many consider the second highway as the most photogenic: the U.S. Highway 101. It traverses the Oregon coast from its northern border with Washington to its southern border with California.

I flew to Portland and then drove about two hours west to the small coastal town of Seaside. There you can pick up U.S. 101 going south. It is 167 miles from Seaside to Florence[51], and I took an entire day driving the coastline, making frequent stops. I spent three more days shooting in and around Florence. As much publicity as the U.S. Highway gets, the drive south on U.S. 101 is just as spectacular. My first stop on the drive south was at Cannon Beach, which is one of the most photographed spots along the coast. When I arrived, it was raining. I had my entire day planned so that I would get to Florence before sunset. I wasn't sure how long I wanted to wait in my car for the rain to stop. I decided to give it thirty minutes.

Twenty-five minutes later, the rain stopped, and I got out of the car and headed to a hill overlooking the beach. It looked like it was about to start raining again. The overcast skies gave an eerie atmosphere. I set up my tripod and took one shot before it started pouring. I immediately grabbed the tripod and camera and sprinted back to the car. Had the weather been better, I would have probably taken thirty-five or forty shots. When I got to the car and looked at my photo, I smiled because the shot was spot-on. I can't ever remember taking just one photo that ended up great. It was the second-best photo I took on this trip.

There is a picture literally at every turn on this highway. It took all I could to keep to my timetable to arrive in Florence before dark. There are hundreds of overlooks along the highway. Each one offering a different perspective of the coastline and the ocean. Traveling south puts the Pacific on the right side of the car and the sun on your left. That allowed me to shoot with the sun at my back as I drove. Some of the best images I took that day were from pullouts along the highway.

There were cliffs with crashing waves, rock formations, beaches, bridges crossing rivers, and lighthouses, all along the way. It was probably the best one-day shooting I had ever done. If you are traveling this highway, don't miss Cannon Beach, Seal Rock, Otter Cove, Yaquina Lighthouse, Sea Lion Caves, Thor's Well, Whale's Cove, Heceta Head Lighthouse, and Neptune Beach.

Just south of Florence, the Oregon coast turns from rugged coastline into sand dunes. It is an amazing transition that can be seen from an overlook at Neptune Beach. I spent a couple of days in and around Florence, shooting waterfalls, rivers and streams, dunes, and covered bridges. It was here that I shot "Sweet Creek." It has been one of my top three award-winning photographs.

You need three days to shoot this area. Best time to shoot: summer.

New River Gorge/Gauley River Recreation Area, West Virginia

This is an excellent location for shooting fall colors and waterfalls. It is in the heartland and West Virginia's coal country. There are great photos to be taken in many of the state parks.

It was here that I shot my best-selling photograph. The image is entitled "Cathedral Falls." It is a waterfall along the road from Charleston, West Virginia to the Gauley River area. It is in fact just past a bridge in the town of Gauley Bridge. I passed it on my way to the area, but it was dark at the time, and I didn't see it. On my way back to Charleston, I passed it during late morning. I had already packed my camera and gear for the flight back home. When I saw the waterfall, I immediately found a place to pull off the road and walked back to the falls. There were lots of kids playing in the pool that had formed at its foot. I was there at least two hours waiting for the kids to move away from the photo I had framed. When I am shooting landscapes, I often have to deal with people who may be in the way of capturing my image. That never bothers me, and I never ask anyone to move. I simply wait for people. I have never missed a photo opportunity doing it that way.

Babcock State Park is a great place to shoot the waterfalls and fall colors and is a working grist mill. There were hundreds of working mills scattered throughout the U.S.[52] Today, there are less than twenty, and only a handful are still working. I had seen the grist mill on Glade Creek in magazines and books and had always been fascinated whenever I saw it. It wasn't until I went to the New River Gorge area on a photo shoot in 2012 that I discovered why.

On the second day of the shoot, I got to the mill early and shot there for almost half the day. You can buy cornmeal ground at the mill in the small gift shop inside. While browsing through the store, I discovered a jigsaw puzzle for sale. When I saw the picture on the puzzle box, I finally realized why that mill somehow was locked in my mind. My mother had been a big jigsaw puzzle fan when we were young. She loved doing her puzzles. When I saw the puzzle of the mill, I instantly had a flashback because it was one of my mother's. She had it on a table in our house on Lodi Point somewhere around 1957. It made my day and made it all come full circle.

You need at least four days to shoot this area. Best time to shoot: spring, summer, and fall.

Notes

Childhood

1. "Clear-channel Station," Wikipedia, last modified February 14, 2022, https://en.wikipedia.org/wiki/Clear-channel_station.

EJ Smoke

1. "Seneca Lake: New York," Wikipedia, last modified January 14, 2022, https://en.wikipedia.org/wiki/Seneca_Lake_(New_York).

Radio Majic

1. "Radio in the United States," Wikipedia, last modified January 1, 2022, https://en.wikipedia.org/wiki/Radio_in_the_United_States.
2. "John R. Brinkley," Wikipedia, last modified December 24, 2021, https://en.wikipedia.org/wiki/John_R._Brinkley.
3. "Communications Act of 1934," Wikipedia, last modified January 2, 2022, https://en.wikipedia.org/wiki/Communications_Act_of_1934#1934:_Commercial_radio_debate.
4. Wikipedia, "John R. Brinkley."
5. Wikipedia, "Communications Act of 1934."
6. "Telecommunications Act of 1996," Wikipedia, last modified November 11, 2021, https://en.wikipedia.org/wiki/Telecommunications_Act_of_1996.
7. "Plugola," Wikipedia, last modified December 1, 2021, https://en.wikipedia.org/wiki/Plugola.
8. "Payola," Wikipedia, last modified February 11, 2022, https://en.wikipedia.org/wiki/Payola.
9. Wikipedia, "Clear-channel Stations."

Houston Radio Makes History

1. "Lee P. Brown," Wikipedia, last modified January 28, 2022, https://en.wikipedia.org/wiki/Lee_P._Brown.

Endings

1. Wikipedia, "Telecommunications Act of 1996."
2. Wikipedia, "Telecommunications Act of 1996."

Again in Radio

1. "About CPB," Corporation for Public Broadcasting, accessed February 8, 2022, https://www.cpb.org/aboutcpb.
2. "Corporation for Public Broadcasting," Wikipedia, last modified February 3, 2022, https://en.wikipedia.org/wiki/Corporation_for_Public_Broadcasting.

Have Camera Will Travel

1. "List of National Parks of the United States," Wikipedia, last modified February 4, 2022, https://en.wikipedia.org/wiki/List_of_national_parks_of_the_United_States.
2. "National Parks Tourism in United States," HiSoUR, accessed February 8, 2022, https://www.hisour.com/national-parks-in-united-states-48895/.
3. Ibid.
4. "Yosemite: Yosemite National Park Celebrates 120th Birthday on October 1," last modified September 20, 2010, National Park Service, https://www.nps.gov/yose/learn/news/yose120.htm.
5. "About America's National Parks," National Park Posters, accessed February 8, 2022, https://national-park-posters.com/products/americas-national-parks-map.
6. "National Parks Tourism in United States," HiSoUR, accessed February 8, 2022, https://www.hisour.com/national-parks-in-united-states-48895/.
7. "How Many National Parks Are There NPS?" FindAnyAnswer.com, accessed February 8, 2022, https://findanyanswer.com/how-many-national-parks-are-there-nps.
8. "Where Is the Biggest National Park?" The Biggest, accessed February 8, 2022, https://bigbangpokemon.com/nature/where-is-the-biggest-national-park.html.
9. "Where Is the Largest State Park in the Continuous US," Bristolpetitions.com, accessed February 8, 2022, https://www.bristolpetitions.com/where-is-the-largest-state-park-in-the-continuous-us/.

10. Wikipedia, "List of National Parks of the United States."
11. Ibid.
12. "Olympic: Wilderness," National Park Service, accessed February 8, 2022, https://www.nps.gov/olym/planyourvisit/wilderness.htm.
13. "Olympic: Discover Olympic's Diverse Wilderness," National Park Service, accessed February 8, 2022, https://www.nps.gov/olym/index.htm.
14. "Acadia National Park," Wikipedia, last modified January 25, 2022, https://en.wikipedia.org/wiki/Acadia_National_Park.
15. "The Park Loop Road," Academia National Park, accessed February 16, 2022, https://acadiamagic.com/park-loop-road.html.
16. "Rocky Mountain National Park," Wikipedia, last modified February 13, 2022, https://en.wikipedia.org/wiki/Rocky_Mountain_National_Park.
17. "Great Smoky Mountains National Park," Chiff.com, accessed February 13, 2022, http://www.chiff.com/travel/smoky-mountains-national-park.htm.
18. "Posts Tagged 'Cherokee North Carolina'," Year Long Adventure, accessed February 13, 2022, https://yearlongadventure.wordpress.com/tag/cherokee-north-carolina/.
19. "Yellowstone National Park," Wikipedia, last modified February 14, 2022, https://en.wikipedia.org/wiki/Yellowstone_National_Park.
20. "Seven Wonders of the World for 2022," Travel Talks Platform, last modified January 3, 2022, https://traveltalksplatform.com/2022/01/03/seven-wonders-of-the-world-for-2022/.
21. Nina Kokotas Hahn, "A Guide to Outsmarting the Crowds at Yellowstone National Park," Conde Nast Traveler, last modified November 7, 2021, https://www.cntraveler.com/story/yellowstone-national-park-guide.
22. "Yellowstone National Park," Wikipedia, last modified August 14, 2022, https://en.wikipedia.org/wiki/Yosemite_National_Park.
23. Kat Eschner, "Lincoln's Signature Laid the Groundwork for the National Park System," Smithsonian Magazine, last modified June 30, 2017, https://www.smithsonianmag.com/smart-news/lincolns-signature-laid-groundwork-national-park-system-180963826/.
24. "Ansel Adams," Wikipedia, last modified February 15, 2022, https://en.wikipedia.org/wiki/Ansel_Adams.
25. "Yosemite: Waterfalls," National Park Service, accessed February 16, 2022, https://www.nps.gov/yose/planyourvisit/waterfalls.htm.
26. "The Most Photo Worthy Waterfalls and Viewpoints at Yosemite," Red Tail Ranch: Bed & Breakfast, accessed February 16, 2022, https://www.red-tail-ranch.com/rtr-blog/the-most-photo-worthy-waterfalls-and-viewpoints-at-yosemite#:~:text=Yosemite%20Falls%20is%20the%20tallest,as%20the%20Empire%20State%20Building.
27. "Pictures: Grand Teton National Park," National Geographic, accessed February 8, 2022, https://www.nationalgeographic.com/travel/article/pictures-grand-teton-national-park.

28. "Grand Teton National Park's Wildlife," Greater Yellowstone Resource Guide, accessed February 13, 2022, http://www.greater-yellowstone.com/Grand-Teton-Park/wildlife.html.
29. "Death Valley: Weather," National Park Service, February 13, 2022, https://www.nps.gov/deva/learn/nature/weather-and-climate.htm.
30. "This Month in Climate History: Earth's Hottest Temperature," National Centers for Environmental Information, accessed February 13, 2022, https://www.ncdc.noaa.gov/news/month-climate-history-earth's-hottest-temperature.
31. Sylas Wright, "The Dynamics of California Weather," The Collegian, last modified December 3, 2004, https://collegian.csufresno.edu/archive/2004/12/3/news/weather.shtml.
32. Kenton Krueger, "Magic & Allure in a Place Called 'Death'," Backcountry Journeys: Photography Tours, Workshops & Safaris, last modified November 22, 2021, https://backcountryjourneys.com/magical-allure-of-a-place-called-death/.
33. "Death Valley: The Lost '49ers," National Park Service, accessed February 16, 2022, https://www.nps.gov/deva/learn/historyculture/the-lost-49ers.htm.
34. Ibid.
35. "Death Valley: Frequently Asked Questions," National Park Service, accessed February 16, 2022, https://www.nps.gov/deva/faqs.htm.
36. Ibid.
37. Ibid.
38. "Death Valley: Twenty Mule Teams," National Park Service, accessed February 16, 2022, https://www.nps.gov/deva/learn/historyculture/twenty-mule-teams.htm.
39. National Park Service, "Death Valley: Frequently Asked Questions."
40. Paul Terry, "Death Valley National Park," The Independent Tourist: Travel Locations and Tips for Independent Travelers, last modified January 18, 2013, https://theindependenttourist.net/tag/death-valley-national-park/.
41. "Crater Lake National Park," Wikipedia, last modified January 25, 2022, https://en.wikipedia.org/wiki/Crater_Lake_National_Park#:~:text=Established%20in%201902%2C%20Crater%20Lake,the%20surrounding%20hills%20and%20forests.
42. Paul Depperschmidt, "Crater Lake – Oregon," Adventures of the Black Pearl, last modified December 16, 2022, https://www.blackpearladventures.com/post/crater-lake-oregon.
43. Wikipedia, "Crater Lake National Park."
44. "Newberry Volcano," Wikipedia, last modified February 9, 2022, https://en.wikipedia.org/wiki/Newberry_Volcano.
45. Wikipedia, "Crater Lake National Park."
46. "Mount Mazama," Wikipedia, last modified February 5, 2022, https://en.wikipedia.org/wiki/Mount_Mazama.
47. Wikipedia, "Crater Lake National Park."
48. Wikipedia, "Crater Lake National Park."

49. *The following story is told from memory. For another version, see here: "Llao," Wikipedia, last modified March 10, 2020, https://en.wikipedia.org/wiki/Llao.
50. Valerie Wheatley, "14 Awesome and Adventurous Things to Do in Hood River, Oregon," Wandering Wheatleys, last modified October 31, 2021, https://wanderingwheatleys.com/best-things-to-do-in-hood-river-oregon/.
51. "Distance from Seaside to Florence on the Oregon Coast," Oregon Coast, accessed February 16, 2022, https://theoregoncoast.info/Distance/Distance-from-Seaside-to-Florence.html.
52. "Woodson's Mill: Historic National Landmark," Nelson County Virginia, accessed February 16, 2022, https://www.nelsoncountyva.org/Woodsons.htm.

Recognitions

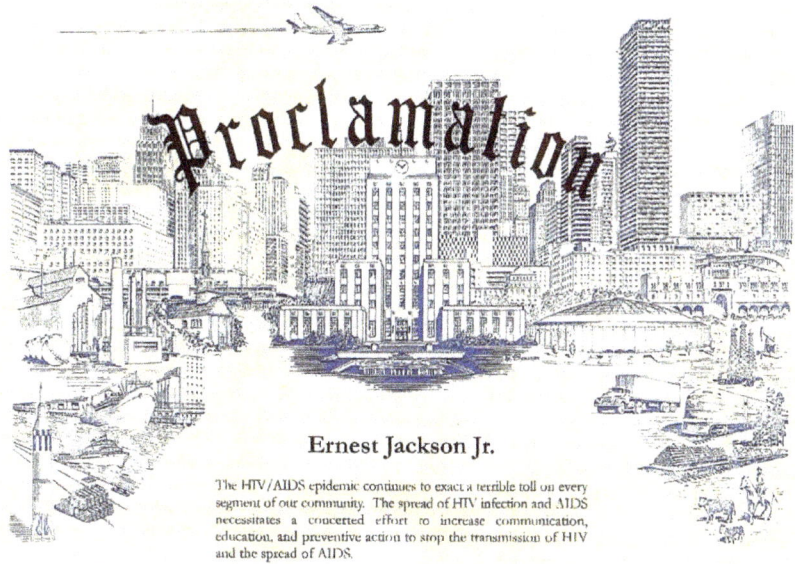

Proclamation

Ernest Jackson Jr.

The HIV/AIDS epidemic continues to exact a terrible toll on every segment of our community. The spread of HIV infection and AIDS necessitates a concerted effort to increase communication, education, and preventive action to stop the transmission of HIV and the spread of AIDS.

Project W.A.V.E. Inc. is a non-profit organization that, in partnership with the private and public sectors, strives to fight the HIV/AIDS epidemic in communities of color. On November 1, 2001, a fund-raising dinner will be held to benefit Project W.A.V.E. Inc. This special event will include a tribute to Ernest Jackson Jr., founder of Project W.A.V.E. Inc.

The City of Houston commends Project W.A.V.E. Inc. and Ernest Jackson Jr. for their efforts to prevent transmission of HIV and the further spread of AIDS, and extends best wishes to all for a successful and rewarding event.

Therefore, I, Lee P. Brown, Mayor of the City of Houston, hereby proclaim November 1, 2001, as

Ernest Jackson Jr. Day

in Houston, Texas.

In Witness Whereof, I have hereunto set my hand and have caused the Official Seal of the City of Houston to be affixed this 1st day of November, 2001, A.D.

Lee P. Brown
Mayor of the City of Houston

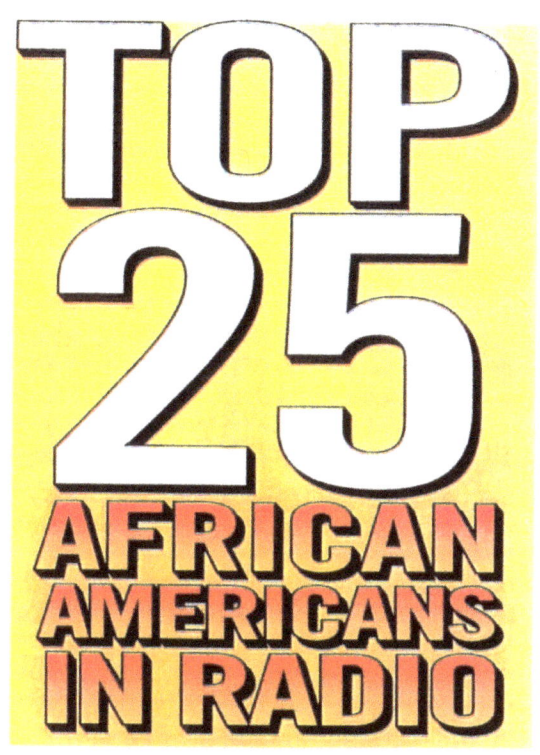

RADIO INK
MARCH 2001

WILLIAM JEFFERSON CLINTON

October 31, 2001

Warm greetings to all those gathered to pay tribute to Ernie Jackson and to support the important mission of Project WAVE.

Since 1999, Project WAVE's unswerving commitment to fighting AIDS globally -- and particularly to combating the epidemic in communities of color -- has been a beacon of hope and an example to many. I commend my good friend, Congresswoman Sheila Jackson Lee, for her investment in this endeavor; she has been a constant advocate and powerful voice on your behalf. Hillary and I join with you all in celebrating her leadership and the outstanding pioneering work of Ernie Jackson and your entire organization.

I look forward to working with you in the months ahead and hope we will have an opportunity to meet soon. Best wishes for a memorable evening.

Bill Clinton

The Senate of The State of Texas

SENATOR RODNEY ELLIS
District 13

PRESIDENT PRO TEMPORE
1999 - 2000

COMMITTEES:

Chair, Finance
Jurisprudence
Redistricting
Legislative Budget Board

November 1, 2001

PROJECT W.A.V.E.
Mr. Ernest Jackson, Jr., President

Dear Ernest:

I would like to personally congratulate you on the magnificent work that you have done in establishing PROJECT W.A.V.E. PROJECT W.A.V.E. is an integral and important part of the work that our community does in the fight against HIV and AIDS.

You have demonstrated that hard work and determination can bring the public and private sectors together to fight the HIV and AIDS epidemic. Your work in Houston is commendable and I have every reason to believe that a national campaign will be as equally successful. Your work in Houston and the rest of the country is deeply appreciated.

I wish you all the best.

Sincerely,

Rodney Ellis

Rodney Ellis

Lyric Centre
440 Louisiana, Suite 575
Houston, Texas 77002
(713) 236-0306
FAX: (713) 236-0604

P.O. Box 12068
Austin, Texas 78711
(512) 463-0113
FAX: (512) 463-0006 • TDD 1-800-735-2989
E-Mail: rodney.ellis@senate.state.tx.us

2440 Texas Parkway, Suite 260
Missouri City, Texas 77489
(281) 261-2360

FAMILY TREE

EARNEST JACKSON JR.
BORN: JANUARY 18, 1943
WICHITA FALLS, TEXAS

MOTHER: ROSIE MAE JACKSON
FATHER: ERNEST JACKSON
GRAND MOTHER: MINNIE BENNETT
GRAND FATHER: LONNIE BENNETT

WIFE: WILLDA SHAW JACKSON
EX WIFE: SHARON WARNER

SONS: TERRY JACKSON
SCOTT JACKSON
MARK JACKSON
BLAKE JACKSON
MATTHEW JACKSON

BROTHER: PATRICK JACKSON
SISTERS: ALMA JONES
NORMA CAIN

NEPHEWS: DARNELL CAIN
DWAYNE CAIN
PATRICK JACKSON JR.
BLAKE JACKSON
JULIAN JACKSON

NIECES: KELLY CAIN
ROSANNE CAIN

GRAND CHILDREN: NATASHA JACKSON
KYLE JACKSON
ERIKA JACKSON
NOLAN JACKSON
PIERCE JACKSON

GRAND NIECES: SHAKARA PERKINS
AIYANA CAIN
CHAYA CAIN

GRAND NEPHEWS: SHAVONTI CAIN
Q'ARON MAYE

GREAT GRAND NEPHEW: KHIMIR MOSES

Certificate of Congressional Recognition
to

Ernest Jackson, Jr.

Founder of
"PROJECT W.A.V.E., INC.
(War against the Virus Escalating)

WHEREAS, Project W.A.V. E., Inc., has continued to be a success under the auspices of Ernest Jackson, Jr., former Vice President & General Manager of KMJQ-FM and KBXX-FM (Majic 102 & 97.9 Box); and

WHEREAS, Currently, approximately 775,000 Americans are infected with the HIV virus and another 216,000 have AIDS; and

WHEREAS, While these statistics are grim, today we pause to focus our attention on the thousands of success stories – individuals who have survived and even prospered despite HIV infection; and

WHEREAS, Project W.A.V.E., Inc. and this Four Step Plan intended to slow the rapid escalating HIV infection rate among Houston's population. This will also show optimism to those newly diagnosed, to overcome the challenges that lay ahead; and

WHEREAS, With Ernest Jackson, Jr., leading the way and standing with PROJECT W.A.V.E., INC., we will eventually win and conquer this dreadful disease; and

NOW, THEREFORE, BE IT RESOLVED that, on behalf of the constituents of the Eighteenth Congressional District of Texas, I join with everyone to pay special tribute to Ernest Jackson, Jr., on this special and important evening. While commemorating Project W.A.V.E., Inc., and the overwhelming success of having other states committed to start with this program as well. I salute every brave person who has battled and beaten this disease.

November 1, 2001

Sheila Jackson Lee
Member of Congress

References

1. "Clear-channel Station," Wikipedia, accessed February 14, 2022, https://en.wikipedia.org/wiki/Clear-channel_station.
2. "Seneca Lake: New York," Wikipedia, last modified January 14, 2022, https://en.wikipedia.org/wiki/Seneca_Lake_(New_York).
3. "Radio in the United States," Wikipedia, last modified January 1, 2022, https://en.wikipedia.org/wiki/Radio_in_the_United_States.
4. "John R. Brinkley," Wikipedia, last modified December 24, 2021, https://en.wikipedia.org/wiki/John_R._Brinkley.
5. "Communications Act of 1934," Wikipedia, last modified January 2, 2022, https://en.wikipedia.org/wiki/Communications_Act_of_1934#1934:_Commercial_radio_debate.
6. "John R. Brinkley," Wikipedia, last modified December 24, 2021, https://en.wikipedia.org/wiki/John_R._Brinkley.
7. "Communications Act of 1934," Wikipedia, last modified January 2, 2022, https://en.wikipedia.org/wiki/Communications_Act_of_1934#1934:_Commercial_radio_debate.
8. "Telecommunications Act of 1996," Wikipedia, last modified November 11, 2021,

https://en.wikipedia.org/wiki/Telecommunications_Act_of_1996.
9. "Plugola," Wikipedia, last modified December 1, 2021, https://en.wikipedia.org/wiki/Plugola.
10. "Payola," Wikipedia, last modified February 11, 2022, https://en.wikipedia.org/wiki/Payola.
11. "Clear-channel Station," Wikipedia, accessed February 14, 2022, https://en.wikipedia.org/wiki/Clear-channel_station.
12. "Lee P. Brown," Wikipedia, last modified January 28, 2022, https://en.wikipedia.org/wiki/Lee_P._Brown.
13. "Telecommunications Act of 1996," Wikipedia, last modified November 11, 2021, https://en.wikipedia.org/wiki/Telecommunications_Act_of_1996.
14. "Telecommunications Act of 1996," Wikipedia, last modified November 11, 2021, https://en.wikipedia.org/wiki/Telecommunications_Act_of_1996.
15. "About CPB," Corporation for Public Broadcasting, accessed February 8, 2022, https://www.cpb.org/aboutcpb.
16. "Corporation for Public Broadcasting," Wikipedia, last modified February 3, 2022, https://en.wikipedia.org/wiki/Corporation_for_Public_Broadcasting.
17. "List of National Parks of the United States," Wikipedia, last modified February 4, 2022, https://en.wikipedia.org/wiki/List_of_national_parks_of_the_United_States.

18. "National Parks Tourism in United States," HiSoUR, accessed February 8, 2022, https://www.hisour.com/national-parks-in-united-states-48895/.
19. "National Parks Tourism in United States," HiSoUR, accessed February 8, 2022, https://www.hisour.com/national-parks-in-united-states-48895/.
20. "Yosemite: Yosemite National Park Celebrates 120th Birthday on October 1," last modified September 20, 2010, National Park Service, https://www.nps.gov/yose/learn/news/yose120.htm.
21. "About America's National Parks," National Park Posters, accessed February 8, 2022, https://national-park-posters.com/products/americas-national-parks-map.
22. "National Parks Tourism in United States," HiSoUR, accessed February 8, 2022, https://www.hisour.com/national-parks-in-united-states-48895/.
23. "How Many National Parks Are There NPS?" FindAnyAnser.com, accessed February 8, 2022, https://findanyanswer.com/how-many-national-parks-are-there-nps.
24. "Where Is the Biggest National Park?" The Biggest, accessed February 8, 2022, https://bigbangpokemon.com/nature/where-is-the-biggest-national-park.html.
25. "Where Is the Largest State Park in the Continuous US," Bristolpetitions.com, accessed February 8, 2022, https://www.bristolpetitions.com/where-is-the-largest-state-park-in-the-continuous-us/.
26. "List of National Parks of the United States," Wikipedia, last modified February 4, 2022, https://en.wikipedia.org/wiki/List_of_national_parks_of_the_United_States.

27. "List of National Parks of the United States," Wikipedia, last modified February 4, 2022, https://en.wikipedia.org/wiki/List_of_national_parks_of_the_United_States.

28. "Olympic: Wilderness," National Park Service, accessed February 8, 2022, https://www.nps.gov/olym/planyourvisit/wilderness.htm.

29. "Olympic: Discover Olympic's Diverse Wilderness," National Park Service, accessed February 8, 2022, https://www.nps.gov/olym/index.htm.

30. "Acadia National Park," Wikipedia, last modified January 25, 2022, https://en.wikipedia.org/wiki/Acadia_National_Park.

31. "The Park Loop Road," Academia National Park, accessed February 16, 2022, https://acadiamagic.com/park-loop-road.html.

32. "Rocky Mountain National Park," Wikipedia, last modified February 13, 2022, https://en.wikipedia.org/wiki/Rocky_Mountain_National_Park.

33. "Great Smoky Mountains National Park," Chiff.com, accessed February 13, 2022, http://www.chiff.com/travel/smoky-mountains-national-park.htm.

34. "Posts Tagged 'Cherokee North Carolina'," Year Long Adventure, accessed February 13, 2022, https://yearlongadventure.wordpress.com/tag/cherokee-north-carolina/.

35. "Yellowstone National Park," Wikipedia, last modified February 14, 2022, https://en.wikipedia.org/wiki/Yellowstone_National_Park.

36. "Seven Wonders of the World for 2022," Travel Talks Platform, last modified January 3, 2022, https://trav-

eltalksplatform.com/2022/01/03/seven-wonders-of-the-world-for-2022/.

37. Nina Kokotas Hahn, "A Guide to Outsmarting the Crowds at Yellowstone National Park," Conde Nast Traveler, last modified November 7, 2021, https://www.cntraveler.com/story/yellowstone-national-park-guide.

38. "Yellowstone National Park," Wikipedia, last modified August 14, 2022, https://en.wikipedia.org/wiki/Yosemite_National_Park.

39. Kat Eschner, "Lincoln's Signature Laid the Groundwork for the National Park System," Smithsonian Magazine, last modified June 30, 2017, https://www.smithsonianmag.com/smart-news/lincolns-signature-laid-groundwork-national-park-system-180963826/.

40. "Ansel Adams," Wikipedia, last modified February 15, 2022, https://en.wikipedia.org/wiki/Ansel_Adams.

41. "Yosemite: Waterfalls," National Park Service, accessed February 16, 2022, https://www.nps.gov/yose/planyourvisit/waterfalls.htm.

42. "The Most Photo Worthy Waterfalls and Viewpoints at Yosemite," Red Tail Ranch: Bed & Breakfast, accessed February 16, 2022, https://www.red-tail-ranch.com/rtr-blog/the-most-photo-worthy-waterfalls-and-viewpoints-at-yosemite#:~:text=Yosemite%20Falls%20is%20the%20tallest,as%20the%20Empire%20State%20Building.

43. "Pictures: Grand Teton National Park," National Geographic, accessed February 8, 2022, https://www.nationalgeographic.com/travel/article/pictures-grand-teton-national-park.

44. "Grand Teton National Park's Wildlife," Greater Yellowstone Resource Guide, accessed February 13, 2022, http://www.greater-yellowstone.com/Grand-Teton-Park/wildlife.html.
45. "Death Valley: Weather," National Park Service, accessed February 13, 2022, https://www.nps.gov/deva/learn/nature/weather-and-climate.htm.
46. "This Month in Climate History: Earth's Hottest Temperature," National Centers for Environmental Information, accessed February 13, 2022, https://www.ncdc.noaa.gov/news/month-climate-history-earth's-hottest-temperature.
47. Sylas Wright, "The Dynamics of California Weather," The Collegian, last modified December 3, 2004, https://collegian.csufresno.edu/archive/2004/12/3/news/weather.shtml.
48. Kenton Krueger, "Magic & Allure in a Place Called 'Death'," Backcountry Journeys: Photography Tours, Workshops & Safaris, last modified November 22, 2021, https://backcountryjourneys.com/magical-allure-of-a-place-called-death/.
49. "Death Valley: The Lost '49ers," National Park Service, accessed February 16, 2022, https://www.nps.gov/deva/learn/historyculture/the-lost-49ers.htm.
50. "Death Valley: The Lost '49ers," National Park Service, accessed February 16, 2022, https://www.nps.gov/deva/learn/historyculture/the-lost-49ers.htm.
51. "Death Valley: Frequently Asked Questions," National Park Service, accessed February 16, 2022, https://www.nps.gov/deva/faqs.htm.

52. "Death Valley: Frequently Asked Questions," National Park Service, accessed February 16, 2022, https://www.nps.gov/deva/faqs.htm.
53. "Death Valley: Frequently Asked Questions," National Park Service, accessed February 16, 2022, https://www.nps.gov/deva/faqs.htm.
54. "Death Valley: Twenty Mule Teams," National Park Service, accessed February 16, 2022, https://www.nps.gov/deva/learn/historyculture/twenty-mule-teams.htm.
55. "Death Valley: Frequently Asked Questions," National Park Service, accessed February 16, 2022, https://www.nps.gov/deva/faqs.htm.
56. Paul Terry, "Death Valley National Park," The Independent Tourist: Travel Locations and Tips for Independent Travelers, last modified January 18, 2013, https://theindependenttourist.net/tag/death-valley-national-park/.
57. "Crater Lake National Park," Wikipedia, last modified January 25, 2022, https://en.wikipedia.org/wiki/Crater_Lake_National_Park#:~:text=Established%20in%201902%2C%20Crater%20Lake,the%20surrounding%20hills%20and%20forests.
58. Paul Depperschmidt, "Crater Lake – Oregon," Adventures of the Black Pearl, last modified December 16, 2022, https://www.blackpearladventures.com/post/crater-lake-oregon.
59. "Crater Lake National Park," Wikipedia, last modified January 25, 2022, https://en.wikipedia.org/wiki/Crater_Lake_National_Park#:~:text=Established

%20in%201902%2C%20Crater%20Lake,the%20surrounding%20hills%20and%20forests.
60. "Newberry Volcano," Wikipedia, last modified February 9, 2022, https://en.wikipedia.org/wiki/Newberry_Volcano.
61. "Crater Lake National Park," Wikipedia, last modified January 25, 2022, https://en.wikipedia.org/wiki/Crater_Lake_National_Park#:~:text=Established %20in%201902%2C%20Crater%20Lake,the%20surrounding%20hills% 20and%20forests.
62. "Mount Mazama," Wikipedia, last modified February 5, 2022, https://en.wikipedia.org/wiki/Mount_Mazama.
63. "Crater Lake National Park," Wikipedia, last modified January 25, 2022, https://en.wikipedia.org/wiki/Crater_Lake_National_Park#:~:text=Established%20in%201902%2C%20Crater%20Lake,the%20surrounding%20hills%20and%20forests.
64. "Crater Lake National Park," Wikipedia, last modified January 25, 2022, https://en.wikipedia.org/wiki/Crater_Lake_National_Park#:~:text=Established%20in%201902%2C%20Crater%20Lake,the%20surrounding%20hills%20and%20forests.
65. "Llao," Wikipedia, last modified March 10, 2020, https://en.wikipedia.org/wiki/Llao.
66. Valerie Wheatley, "14 Awesome and Adventurous Things to Do in Hood River, Oregon," Wandering Wheatleys, last modified October 31, 2021, https://wanderingwheatleys.com/best-things-to-do-in-hood-river-oregon/.

67. "Distance from Seaside to Florence on the Oregon Coast," Oregon Coast, accessed February 16, 2022, https://theoregoncoast.info/Distance/Distance-from-Seaside-to-Florence.html.
68. "Woodson's Mill: Historic National Landmark," Nelson County Virginia, accessed February 16, 2022, https://www.nelsoncountyva.org/Woodsons.htm.

www.ingramcontent.com/pod-product-compliance
Lightning Source LLC
Chambersburg PA
CBHW061728070526
44583CB00024B/3051